DISCIPLE

UNDER THE TREE OF LIFE

Teacher Helps

The Writings • John • Revelation

For more information about DISCIPLE or DISCIPLE training seminars, call toll free 800-251-8591 or 800-672-1789.

Cover design by **Mary M. Johannes**.

Nellie M. Moser, Senior Editor; Mark Price, Development Editor; Katherine C. Bailey, Production Editor; Linda O. Spicer, Secretary; Ed Wynne, Design Manager.

02 03 04 05 06 07 08 09 10 —10 9 8 7 6 5 4 3 2

Contents

Put the Study Manual to Work

Each part of the study manual has a specific function both in daily preparation and in the weekly group meeting.

Theme Word

The theme word gives a clue to the subject of the lesson and the Scripture studied in the lesson.
- Display the word during each group meeting.
- Suggest persons connect the theme word with the lesson title as a reminder of the themes unique to the books of the Writings and of the message of John and Revelation.

Theme Verse(s)

The theme verse(s) expresses the lesson focus and might be read during "Gathering and Prayer."

Title

The titles are descriptive of situations, conditions, or content and illustrate the variety in the study's Scripture.

Our Human Condition

"Our Human Condition" is a statement of *who we are* as human beings. "Marks of Faithful Community" is the faith community's response to "Our Human Condition," arrived at by viewing "Our Human Condition" through Scripture. These two sections always are viewed together.

Assignment

Disciplined daily study of Scripture is central to DISCIPLE: UNDER THE TREE OF LIFE.
- The "Assignment" section indicates when to read the week's Scripture and when to read the study manual and write the responses called for.
- Insist on daily notetaking along with daily Scripture reading. The second page of each lesson in the manual provides space for notes—information and insights gleaned from Scripture and questions about the Scripture. Many activities in the weekly session call for use of the notes in group discussion and interaction.
- Invite the group to covenant together to prepare this weekly page of notes.
- Challenge group members through your own example of daily reading, study, and notetaking.
- Make use of the work persons have done during the week. The extent to which you recognize and use the preparation group members have made will determine the degree of commitment they continue to bring to completing assignments.

Psalm of the Week

The "Psalm of the Week" intends to lead participants into a deeper life of prayer, using Psalms as a guide. The "Psalm of the Week" is prayed aloud daily during study and used in each group session.

Prayer

The prayer psalm printed in the manual is a starting point for personal prayer.
- Encourage persons to jot down group and scriptural concerns about which to pray daily.
- Establish a plan for group members to pray for one another.

Fruit From the Tree of Life

This section comments on the Scripture and draws meaning from it.
- Write notes in the margin as you read and during discussion in the group meeting.
- Decide how to hear the information persons write in the blanks in this section. Some information will be suited to response on a voluntary basis, some in pairs or in threes or in the entire group.

Marks of Faithful Community

"Marks of Faithful Community" identifies beliefs, attitudes, and actions of faithful community. Notice that "Marks of Faithful Community" does not include the word *the* before the word *faithful*. Faithful community is not an institution but a way of *being*. The mark of faithful community that appears in the margin beside this section always begins *"Being faithful community, we . . ."*
- Make the connection between "Marks of Faithful Community" and "Our Human Condition."

The Radical Disciple

"The Radical Disciple" focuses on thoughts or actions relevant to the weekly theme that require stretch in terms of commitment to discipleship. "The Radical Disciple" section appears at different places in the study manual format. Its emphasis determines where it is placed in each lesson. The content varies—sometimes calling for action, other times calling for reflection.

If You Want to Know More

This section invites, but does not require, additional individual study and research.
- Most of what persons learn they can contribute in small group discussions. Occasionally, a brief report to the whole group may be in order.

Weekly Group Schedule and Procedure

Teacher helps for each of the thirty-two group meetings (pages 28–63) follow this format. Copy the planning sheet on page 6 (page 7 for youth) to use in writing your weekly group plan. In the parentheses, beside the designated times, write the clock time you are to begin that part of the session.

GATHERING AND PRAYER

(5 minutes)

Begin on time with those who are there. Use the theme word, theme verse, title, "Our Human Condition," and prayer from the study manual.

VIDEO SEGMENT

(20 minutes) *

The video segment provides persons a common body of information to which to react and focuses attention on the subject of the group meeting.

Teacher helps for each session
• suggest a way to prepare group members to view the video segment;
• provide a summary of the ideas in the segment;
• suggest questions that allow persons to discuss what they have heard.

Preview the video segment before the weekly meeting. * **Notice that in this study some segments are considerably longer than others. So occasionally the time given to this and other parts of the weekly procedure is adjusted to allow time for the longer videos.**

Encourage notetaking during the viewing.

After the discussion, use one of the summary ideas to help group members make connections between the video content and what they have read in the Bible and study manual.

To save time in setting up for the next session, don't rewind the tape.

SCRIPTURE AND STUDY MANUAL

(50 minutes adults)   (35 minutes youth)

Much discussion and activity during this time results from the reading and study persons have done and from their notes and questions.

Allow time in every session for persons to talk about the Scripture they have read. Encourage them to use their notes in the discussion.

This section in the weekly group meeting plan includes a variety of activities for responding to the Scripture for the week. Decide how much time to allot to each activity and when the group will work

and discuss in pairs, threes or fours, or occasionally in the total group.

As you prepare to guide this part of the session, plan activities that make use of group members' preparation.

BREAK

(10 minutes)

Stay within the allotted time. Limit refreshments to a beverage.

ENCOUNTER THE WORD

(40 minutes adults)   (20 minutes youth)

This time focuses on group study of a passage selected from the assigned Scripture. Group members will have read the passage but will not have studied it in detail. No mention of this activity is made in the study manual, and group members will not know before the meeting what passage they will be studying together.

Teacher helps for each session indicate the passage selected for study and one or more study approaches. Most of the approaches are described in detail in *Teaching the Bible to Adults and Youth,* by Dick Murray (Abingdon Press, 1993).
• Familiarize yourself with the suggested approach.
• Test the approach with the selected passage.
• Identify the steps to follow in guiding the study.

MARKS OF FAITHFUL COMMUNITY

(20 minutes)

At this point in the session, you will consider what characterizes faithful community. Draw on the work persons have done in this section of the study manual and on group study and discussion.

The mark of faithful community for each lesson is stated in both the study manual and the teacher helps. Teacher helps emphasize the importance of making the connection between the mark of faithful community and "Our Human Condition" stated at the beginning of the lesson.

Being faithful community is the point of this section and the point of DISCIPLE: UNDER THE TREE OF LIFE. Watch time carefully throughout the session to have the time necessary for this section.

CLOSING AND PRAYER

(5 minutes adults)   (10 minutes youth)
Close the session on time with a prayer or song.

Group Meeting Plan (Adult)
Lesson _____ Title _____

GATHERING AND PRAYER

(5 minutes)   (   )

VIDEO SEGMENT

* (minutes)   (   )
Presenter(s):

Prepare to View Video

View Video
Summary of video content:

BREAK

(10 minutes)   (   )

ENCOUNTER THE WORD

* (minutes)   (   )
Scripture selection:

Discuss After Viewing Video

MARKS OF FAITHFUL COMMUNITY

(20 minutes)   (   )

SCRIPTURE AND STUDY MANUAL

* (minutes)   (   )

CLOSING AND PRAYER

(5 minutes)   (   )

Group Meeting Plan (Youth)
Lesson _____ Title _____

GATHERING AND PRAYER

(5 minutes)   (   )

VIDEO SEGMENT

* (minutes)   (   )
Presenter(s):

Prepare to View Video

BREAK

(10 minutes)   (   )

View Video
Summary of video content:

ENCOUNTER THE WORD

* (minutes)   (   )
Scripture selection:

Discuss After Viewing Video

MARKS OF FAITHFUL COMMUNITY

(20 minutes)   (   )

SCRIPTURE AND STUDY MANUAL

* (minutes)   (   )

CLOSING AND PRAYER

(10 minutes)   (   )

About the Videotapes

Video Opening and Introduction

Each video segment begins with music and an image of the tree framed by moving water. The tree and the water remain constant—just as they do in Scripture. A series of images flows past the tree. Images in the opening for Segments 1 through 16 are appropriate to the Writings. Images in the opening for Segments 17 through 32 are appropriate to John and Revelation. Watch for connections of the images to the Scriptures studied and to the recurring images of the tree and the water.

The host introduces each segment and occasionally provides a follow-up comment.

Video Set

The tree is the focal point of the set for the video presenters. Segments often open and conclude under the tree—just as the Scriptures do. Behind the tree are mountains. And in some segments, a river or sea appears nearby. If you look and listen carefully, you'll see and hear the running water of the stone well in every segment.

The set also includes an interior room with walls and windows. The room's decorations change according to the subject of the video presentation.

The Persian Empire (sixth to fourth centuries B.C.), which stretched from India in the east to Macedonia in the west, is the context for most of the Writings: Esther, Daniel, Ezra, and Nehemiah, for example. To reflect the rich and colorful ornamentation of the Persian period, cloths of gold, blue, red, olive, and brown drape windows, tables, and walls; baskets and bowls of pomegranates, figs, nuts, and leeks sit on the tables; pottery, brass, pillows, and scarves adorn the walls and benches.

During the New Testament segments, the room reflects the simpler interior of a Palestinian home of Jesus' time. Everyday objects—bread, a lamp, water jars, fruit, or herbs—often are the focus of the room.

Host and Presenter Identification

Here is brief biographical information about the host and presenters. More detailed information appears on the back of the videotape case.

Host: Peter Storey—Professor, Practice of Christian Ministry, The Divinity School, Duke University

Presenters
Segment 1: Amy-Jill Levine—E. Rhodes and Leona B. Carpenter Professor of New Testament Studies, Vanderbilt Divinity School

Segment 2: Leslie C. Allen—Professor of Old Testament, Fuller Theological Seminary

Segment 3: Cheryl B. Anderson—Assistant Professor of Old Testament Interpretation, Garrett-Evangelical Theological Seminary

Segment 4: Jin Hee Han—Professor of Biblical Studies, New York Theological Seminary

Segment 5: Sidnie White Crawford—Associate Professor of Hebrew Bible and Chair, Classics and Religious Studies, University of Nebraska-Lincoln

Segment 6: David A. deSilva—Associate Professor of New Testament and Greek, Ashland Theological Seminary

Segment 7: Raymond C. Van Leeuwen—Professor of Biblical Studies, Eastern College

Segment 8: Deborah A. Appler—Assistant Professor of Old Testament, Moravian Theological Seminary

Segment 9: Samuel Pagán—President of Evangelical Seminary of Puerto Rico

Segment 10: W. Sibley Towner—Professor of Biblical Interpretation, Union Theological Seminary and Presbyterian School of Christian Education

Segments 11 and 12: Carol A. Newsom—Professor of Old Testament, Candler School of Theology, Emory University

Segment 13: Ellen F. Davis—Associate Professor of Bible and Practical Theology, The Divinity School, Duke University

Segment 14: Kenneth A. Kanter—Senior Rabbi of Congregation Micah, Nashville, Tennessee

Dancer, Segments 14, 15, 16: Diana Brown Holbert—Pastor of ArtSpirit, a ministry to the arts community of Dallas, Texas

Segment 15: Michael Jinkins—Associate Professor of Pastoral Theology, Austin Presbyterian Theological Seminary

Segment 16: John C. Holbert—Lois Craddock Perkins Professor of Homiletics, Perkins School of Theology, Southern Methodist University

Segment 17: Ben Witherington, III—Professor of New Testament, Asbury Theological Seminary

Segment 18: Marianne Meye Thompson—Professor of New Testament Interpretation, Fuller Theological Seminary

Segment 19: Richard B. Hays—Professor of New Testament, The Divinity School, Duke University

Segment 20: D. Moody Smith, Jr.—George Washington Ivey Professor of New Testament, The Divinity School, Duke University

Segment 21: Sharon H. Ringe—Professor of New Testament, Wesley Theological Seminary

Segment 22: Koo Yong Na—Senior Pastor of the Korean Community Church of New Jersey—United Methodist in Leonia, New Jersey, and Adjunct Professor of Preaching, Drew Theological School

Segment 23: R. Alan Culpepper—Dean of the McAfee School of Theology, Mercer University

Segment 24: R. Grace Jones Imathiu—Senior Pastor of First United Methodist Church, Green Bay, Wisconsin

Segment 25: Charles H. Talbert—Distinguished Professor of Religion, Baylor University

Segment 26: Zan W. Holmes, Jr.—Pastor of St. Luke Community United Methodist Church in Dallas, Texas, and Adjunct Professor of Preaching, Perkins School of Theology

Segment 27: M. Eugene Boring—J. Wylie and Elizabeth M. Briscoe Professor of New Testament at Brite Divinity School, Texas Christian University

Scripture, Segments 27, 28, 29, and 30: Marquis Laughlin— Actor for the Fellowship for the Performing Arts

Segment 28: Catherine Gunsalus González—Professor of Church History, Columbia Theological Seminary

Segment 29: Leonard Thompson—Professor Emeritus of Religious Studies, Lawrence University

Segment 30: Justo L. González—Retired ministerial member of the Rio Grande Conference of The United Methodist Church

Segment 32: Richard B. Wilke—Bishop in Residence at Southwestern College, co-writer of DISCIPLE: UNDER THE TREE OF LIFE study manual

Julia K. Wilke—Volunteer in the church, Sunday school teacher and speaker, co-writer of DISCIPLE: UNDER THE TREE OF LIFE study manual

—————Session 31—————
The Revelation: A Worship Experience

Dennis Parlato—Experienced in film, television, and theater; worship leader of *The Revelation: A Worship Experience*

Mac Pirkle—President of Southern Stage Productions, a theatrical production company, Nashville, Tennessee; writer and creative director of *The Revelation: A Worship Experience*

Don Saliers—Parker Professor of Theology and Worship, Candler School of Theology, Emory University; consultant and co-writer on the liturgical moments in *The Revelation: A Worship Experience*

The following DISCIPLE churches provided a spoken greeting from Revelation 1:4 for *The Revelation: A Worship Experience:* Belle-Terrace Presbyterian Church, Augusta, Georgia; Childwall Valley Methodist Church, Liverpool, England; Emory United Methodist Church, Washington, DC; First United Methodist Church, Lawrenceville, Georgia; First United Methodist Church, McAllen, Texas; First United Methodist Church, Richardson, Texas; Hyde Park United Methodist Church, Tampa, Florida; Mississippi Boulevard Christian Church, Memphis, Tennessee; Munholland United Methodist Church, Metairie, Louisiana; Ousley United Methodist Church, Lithonia, Georgia; Paya Lebar Chinese Methodist Church, Singapore; Rosefield Uniting Church, Highgate, South Australia; Roswell United Methodist Church, Roswell, Georgia; St. Agnes' Anglican Church, North Vancouver, British Columbia, Canada; St. Luke's United Methodist Church, Houston, Texas; St. Mark's United Methodist Church, Sacramento, California; Third Baptist Church, Chicago, Illinois.

Video Segment Viewing Times

Because the length of the videos in this study varies from session to session, the time allotments in the weekly session plan for the "Video Segment" section also vary. To accommodate this variety, occasionally the "Video Segment" time is increased by five or ten minutes and the times for "Scripture and Study Manual" and/or "Encounter the Word" sections are adjusted. Always check all time allotments in the weekly session plans.

TAPE 1

Video Segment 1: 12 minutes

Video Segment 2: 13 minutes

Video Segment 3: 11 minutes

Video Segment 4: 14 minutes

Video Segment 5: 13 minutes

Video Segment 6: 12 minutes

Video Segment 7: 11 minutes

Video Segment 8: 11 minutes

TAPE 2

Video Segment 9: 8 minutes

Video Segment 10: 11 minutes

Video Segment 11: 11 minutes

Video Segment 12: 12 minutes

Video Segment 13: 12 minutes

Video Segment 14: 14 minutes

Video Segment 15: 17 minutes

Video Segment 16: 13 minutes

TAPE 3

Video Segment 17: 10 minutes

Video Segment 18: 11 minutes

Video Segment 19: 14 minutes

Video Segment 20: 12 minutes

Video Segment 21: 13 minutes

Video Segment 22: 12 minutes

Video Segment 23: 15 minutes

Video Segment 24: 10 minutes

TAPE 4

Video Segment 25: 15 minutes

Video Segment 26: 11 minutes

Video Segment 27: 18 minutes

Video Segment 28: 13 minutes

Video Segment 29: 13 minutes

Video Segment 30: 14 minutes

Video Segment 32: 18 minutes

TAPE 5

The Revelation: A Worship Experience
Session 31: 86 minutes

The Revelation: A Worship Experience

The Revelation: A Worship Experience, a ninety-minute video designed to be used in DISCIPLE: UNDER THE TREE OF LIFE Session 31, challenges DISCIPLE participants to go beyond familiar notions of the book of Revelation—to come to see

- that God is in control
- that the book of Revelation addresses the church today as it did the early church
- that worship of God is Revelation's answer to a church that has accommodated to the culture and a society whose allegiance is to idols
- that a comfortable church may be unable to recognize the significance of God's victory
- that in any authentic experience of worship the worshiper is confronted by God

Worship plays a central role in the book of Revelation. Through this Revelation video, UNDER THE TREE OF LIFE participants will experience the book of Revelation as worship. Not a worship *service* in the sense of structured formal liturgy but a worship *experience* that evokes awe, praise, and confession, and delivers the "sermon" in unexpected words and images; a worship experience in which the viewer confronts self and is confronted by God; a worship experience that anticipates the certain triumph of God and God's people.

DISCIPLE Participants Equipped

All participants in DISCIPLE: UNDER THE TREE OF LIFE will have studied DISCIPLE: BECOMING DISCIPLES THROUGH BIBLE STUDY, and many will have studied all three earlier phases of DISCIPLE. So they come to this video-led worship experience with knowledge and memory of the biblical story—Genesis to Revelation. And having just completed five weeks of reading and discussing the whole book of Revelation, they come with heightened sensitivity to words and images, to language and symbols. They come equipped with a vocabulary of imagery that both reveals and remains mystery. And even when the language is confusing and the symbols beyond imagining, their experience of Revelation's majesty and mystery invites awe rather than analysis.

A Feast for the Senses

The Revelation: A Worship Experience offers a feast for the senses: music ranging from traditional hymns to original compositions—at times lyrical, at other times upbeat; colorful Revelation-inspired art from the Middle Ages to the twentieth century; symbols and visions of Revelation—fast-moving and ever-changing, at once mysterious and full of meaning, disturbing and comforting, painful and hopeful.

As in any worship experience, participants sing, speak, listen, pray, lament. The video worship leader gives direction and invites participation, narrates the action with words from Revelation, and speaks his own thoughts.

About the Video

The DISCIPLE: UNDER THE TREE OF LIFE videotape set includes five videotapes: Tape 1, Segments 1–8; Tape 2, Segments 9–16; Tape 3, Segments 17–24; Tape 4, Segments 25–30 and 32; Tape 5, Session 31. This video, labeled *The Revelation: A Worship Experience,* guides an interactive worship experience of the book of Revelation. It is integral to Session 31 and is designed to be viewed as the conclusion to that session.

Preview the Video

Previewing the video prior to Session 31 is essential. The video is approximately 90 minutes long, so allow plenty of uninterrupted time to preview it.

As the DISCIPLE group leader, your role during the showing of the video is to assist the video worship leader. Take your cues for initiating group participation from the video worship leader. The group will follow your lead. Few additional instructions are necessary. The video stays on during the entire worship experience.

Use the following information on sequence of group participation to guide your preview of the video. Make note of times and ways you are to lead the group in a response. Be alert to those times the video worship leader indicates you are to take the lead. Pay attention to how the graphics on screen determine pacing of the responses.

Sequence of DISCIPLE Group Participation During the Revelation Video

1. **Scripture.** Group reads Revelation 1:4-8 from the video screen along with the video worship leader. The pace is brisk. Help the group match the pace of the video worship leader.
2. **Doxology.** Sing the Doxology.
3. **Candles.** Group leader lights seven candles as video worship leader lights candles on screen. Pace on screen allows plenty of time for lighting.
4. **Letter.** Group leader breaks the seal on the letter, reads the greeting (church name and location) and the two lines that follow, passes the letter to the next person who reads the next

lines, and so on until the whole letter is read. No need to rush. Each passing of the letter is indicated on the screen by hands passing the letter. The group may match its pace to the passing of the letter on screen.

5. **Lamentations.** After the video worship leader finishes his lamentation, the group leader speaks his or her own lamentation. Begin with either "*I remember with a broken heart*" or "*I remember with tearful eyes.*" Group leader invites participants to speak their lamentations. A puzzle taking form on the screen takes four minutes to complete. If the group finishes early, wait for puzzle to complete.

6. **Pleas for mercy.** Group repeats the phrase "*Have mercy upon us*" with the video worship leader. Group leader then makes her or his own plea for mercy using the words "*Please Lord*" or "*Dear Lord,*" and group responds "*Have mercy upon us.*" Participants make individual pleas for mercy to which the group responds "*Have mercy upon us.*" Again a puzzle forming on the screen takes four minutes to complete.

7. **Lord's Prayer, first part.** Group speaks the first, second, and third petitions following the lead of the video worship leader. Group leader initiates the reading along with the video worship leader.

8. **Lord's Prayer, complete.** Participants pray the Lord's Prayer at their own pace, not trying to recite the prayer in unison. Only 45 seconds are allotted for this praying so the group leader will need to start the praying quickly.

9. **Responsive reading.** Group repeats as instructed, "*Amen. Come, Lord Jesus!*" Repeat again as instructed. No prompt is given by the video worship leader for the third and fourth times the group is expected to repeat the words.

10. **Declaration.** Group leader states name and makes declaration, "*My name is _____ , and I am on a journey to the New Jerusalem in the company of saints.*" Group responds, "*The grace of the Lord Jesus be with you and all the saints. Amen.*" Repeat the pattern for each participant. Words for both the declaration and the response are on the screen. This sequence lasts three minutes and is marked by pictures of saints and martyrs through the ages. The larger the television screen, the better the readability here.

11. **Go in silence.**

Further Information

To avoid fatigue of sitting for ninety minutes, invite the group to stand two or three times for their responses. Three possible times are during the reading of the letter, during the lamentations, and during the pleas for mercy. Standing close in a semicircle makes hearing one another easy, while also having a clear view of the television screen. Arrange the chairs to facilitate both sitting and standing.

DISCIPLE groups come to Session 31 well-rehearsed in expressing personal laments and pleas for mercy, because they will have had opportunity throughout the study for such expression.

Order the Letter

Early in the video, the worship leader indicates that the revelation of Jesus Christ to John has come to the DISCIPLE group in the form of a letter.

Because the letter is personalized, that is, the greeting addresses the particular church of the particular DISCIPLE group, it is not shipped with other DISCIPLE materials. You must order the letter a few weeks before it is to be used in Session 31. The cost of the letter is already covered in the cost of the DISCIPLE materials, but the letter will not be sent to you until you order it.

Each DISCIPLE group needs its own sealed letter. Each DISCIPLE leader has responsibility to order the letter in time to receive it for use in Session 31. Reminders to order the letter appear several times in the teacher helps beginning with Session 17.

Procedure for the Letter

1. Keep in mind that at least two weeks' time is necessary between the time an order is placed and the time the letter is received.

2. Order the *DISCIPLE: UNDER THE TREE OF LIFE Revelation Video Letter* from the DISCIPLE office (800-251-8591, extension 6068) no later than Session 28. Request that the letter be sent directly to you, not to the church; this step will avoid the letter's inadvertently being misplaced or misdirected.

3. The letter will arrive in a mailing tube. Open the tube to check the condition of the letter. BUT DO NOT BREAK THE SEAL ON THE LETTER. The letter should remain rolled up and sealed until time for use in Session 31.

4. If you have problems receiving the letter or if it arrives damaged or if you have questions about its use, contact the DISCIPLE office by telephone using the number above.

Notes

Gather the Candles

The video calls for lighting seven candles symbolizing the seven lampstands or churches in Revelation. Choose candles tall enough and substantial enough to burn for an hour and a half—for example, seven ten-inch white tapers or seven tall white pillar candles. The tapers will require candlesticks; most pillar candles do not require candlesticks. You will need an additional small taper and matches to use in lighting the candles following the procedure on the video. Check the wicks of the candles in advance to make sure they will light properly.

Arrange for the Room

The impact of the video worship experience may be enhanced by arranging to view the video in a place different from where you conduct the weekly study and discussion that precedes the video. The ideal would be to use two different rooms. Providing a different room for viewing the video allows transition both in terms of space and mood from study to worship and allows persons to experience the furnishings of worship—a cloth-draped table holding the seven candles, the semicircle of chairs, and the television monitor—in the moment approaching worship.

• If your group meets regularly in a room at the church, arrange for a second room. If you meet regularly in a home and gather in a room around the television, consider conducting the study and discussion part of the weekly session in another part of the house, leaving the television room available for the Revelation video worship experience.

• Because the visual impact of this video is central to the experience, the size of the television screen is important. Use a television monitor with as large a screen as possible.

• Arrange the chairs in a semicircle so everyone has a close and clear view of the television screen.

• Place the candles on a cloth-draped table in easy view of the group, but to the side of the television screen to minimize glare. Put the matches and a small white taper on the table for use in lighting the candles. If your meeting room has a smoke alarm, consider where best to place the candles.

• Wherever your group meets to view the video, maintain a level of lighting that allows the group to read the letter as it is passed. The candles alone will not provide enough light to read the letter.

• Detailed instructions for preparing to use the video in Session 31 appear on teacher helps pages 60–61.

The Love Feast

This three-fold worship experience in Session 32 follows closely the form and ritual of the traditional love feast of the Church of the Brethren. It has three parts: footwashing, fellowship meal, Holy Communion.

The table is a central symbol of the love feast, for all three parts have their origin at table and their example remembered at table. And each part—washing of feet, eating a meal in fellowship, sharing in the new covenant with bread and cup—is considered a feast. Think of the love feast as a table offering a banquet to all who participate.

The Footwashing

Create an atmosphere of quiet reverence for the footwashing. If you wish to heighten the symbolism of the table, use the same table for each part of the love feast. Arrange a semicircle of chairs facing the cloth-covered table. Place the basin, pitchers of water, and towels on the table for use during the service. Space the chairs far enough apart and back from the table to allow easy movement by each participant. Candles or a dimly-lit room may also contribute to a sense of worship. But keep the room light enough for persons to read easily from their study manual or Bible, and to read the words of hymns.

Following the footwashing, everybody helps remove the basin, pitchers, and towels and prepare the same table for the fellowship meal.

Provide warm water and fresh towels for washing hands before the meal.

Another setup option would be to arrange one area of the room for the footwashing and another for the fellowship and Communion meals. Set up the table for eating and Communion ahead of time with its own chairs and away from the footwashing area.

In planning room arrangement and furniture, take into account persons who may not be able to kneel or stoop.

Fellowship Meal

Keep both the setting and the menu simple. Prepare the table with a cloth, necessary eating utensils, and perhaps a white Christ candle that could also be used on the table during the Communion meal to follow. Serving one another in the act of passing food continues the spirit of the love feast, so plan for seated serving rather than serving buffet style.

A menu of stew or soup, bread, fruit, and beverage or bread, cheese, fruit, olives, nuts, and beverage, or something similar would be appropriate. Planning a meal that does not require cooking would be an advantage in most settings. Make provision for persons with special dietary needs.

When the food is on the table and all are seated, continue the love feast order of service in the study manual. The meal may be eaten in silent reflection or in talking with one another about your experiences of study together.

When the meal is finished, work together to clear the table and make it ready for Holy Communion. The preparation may be done in silence or while singing hymns. When all are seated around the table, continue the love feast order of service for Holy Communion.

Holy Communion

Prepare the elements for the Communion meal in advance. Use traditional unleavened bread, a flat bread such as pita, or an unsliced loaf of bread that can be broken. The common cup, a traditional symbol of unity, may hold the juice for dipping the bread.

If your church requires that ordained clergy administer the sacrament of Holy Communion, and your group does not include an ordained person, ask a member of the clergy to bless the elements ahead of time so the group can proceed with the Communion meal.

Pass the elements so each person serves and is served with both bread and cup.

After the "Sending Forth" at the close of the Communion meal, work together to set the room in order, putting away hymnals, chairs, and tables, and cleaning up the utensils from the fellowship meal.

Psalm of the Week

The "Psalm of the Week" intends to lead people into a deeper life of prayer, using Psalms as a guide. Participants will pray aloud the "Psalm of the Week" daily as they study and weekly in the group session. The Psalms are the hymns and prayers of a community, so whether praying as individuals or as a group, participants will be speaking the words on behalf of and within the community.

Praying the "Psalm of the Week," participants will at times give voice to words that may not match their own feelings or situation. But as the practice of praying continues, they will find themselves discovering fresh meaning in words once thought unrelated to them or their community. Through praying the "Psalm of the Week" over the course of the study, participants will enter into a new relationship with the psalmist, the psalmist's community, and with God.

1. For thirty-two weeks, every day, every week, we will live in the Psalms. We will join our voices with the faith community that stretches across the centuries and reaches around the world. Pray Psalm 146 aloud each day this week.

2. As you read Psalm 132 aloud daily, think about your congregation and your place of worship. Recall the people who made possible your place of worship. Say a prayer for those who prepare it weekly for worship. Picture in your mind and offer thanks for people who passed on to you both a place and a heritage of faith.

3. As you pray Psalm 85 aloud daily, reflect on the needs both communal and individual that call for such a prayer. Pray the prayer as your congregation's prayer to God. What is being asked? What is being acknowledged? Why does your faith congregation need this prayer?

4. As you pray Psalm 126 aloud daily, imagine creative ways to express its sense of joy—perhaps through dance, a drawing, or a banner. Find a hymnal with the song "Bringing In the Sheaves." Consider the words. What is the seed for sowing? the harvest reaped? the cause for rejoicing?

5. Keep Esther's people in mind as you pray Psalm 83 aloud daily. While the psalmist names nations and people threatening Israel in his day, call to mind the many forms of persecution Jews have faced down through history. Pray daily for Israel and its neighbors now that they may achieve a peace beneficial to all.

6. Let Psalm 9 guide you in praying for the nations of the world. As you pray the psalm aloud, let the verses suggest to you needs of particular nations. Keep a balance in your view of nations as you pray for judgment, mercy, justice.

7. In Psalm 1, the righteous are compared to trees and the wicked to chaff. As you read Psalm 1 aloud on Days 1–4, think about what other images might replace *trees* and *chaff* and still carry the psalm's message. Make note of characteristics of trees and chaff. On Days 5–6, rewrite the psalm, replacing *trees* and *chaff* with other images.

8. Each day choose a path and pray Psalm 25 aloud as you walk it. Or if you have access to a labyrinth (a circle design used for meditative walking), pray the psalm as you walk the labyrinth.

9. In Psalm 39 the psalmist puts into words what we have often thought: Life goes by too quickly. As you read the psalm aloud daily, talk back, raise questions, speak your mind—either aloud or with paper and pen.

10. Pray Psalm 90 aloud daily. Each day choose a verse or a line and meditate on it all day. Write it on a sticky note and put it where you will see it. Memorize 90:17 and pray it as you begin work each day.

11. Recognizing that basic injustices do exist, pray Psalm 17 aloud daily for yourself and also on behalf of others. Recall your own experiences of injustice, your sense of things being unfair. Each day think of someone who needs deliverance of some kind, who needs justice. Plead that person's cause as you pray the psalm aloud.

12. We are trying to live in the psalms. Pray Psalm 102 aloud daily and reflect on what it means to live in a psalm, parts of which may not connect with your experience at the moment. Be aware of whether the words strike you differently each day.

13. As you pray Psalm 84 aloud daily, reflect on the similarities in the feelings of joy and anticipation associated with being in the presence of God and being in the presence of the lover. Consider ways love grows—the more it is expressed to God, the more it is expressed to the lover.

14. Pray Psalm 103 aloud daily. As you pray, picture others in your group who also are praying it. Pause to reflect as verses and sections remind you of situations in your own life or in the life of your faith community.

15. Pray Psalm 143 aloud daily. Make the psalm your own. Each day name your enemy—cancer cells, tension in the family, depression, insecurity about the future. Keep the enemy in mind as you pray.

16. Psalm 100 calls all nations to praise the Lord. Pray Psalm 100 aloud daily with a globe or world map in view, calling on different countries and areas of the world by name to praise the Lord.

17. Each day's assignment calls for reading John 1:1-18 and the psalm of the week aloud. On Day 1 read aloud Psalm 33 followed by John 1:1-18. On subsequent days alternate the sequence of reading. Think about the question, What does the Word/word of God make happen?

18. Pray Psalm 24 aloud. Reflect on the condition of your heart and hands as you approach God daily in worship.

19. Pray Psalm 65 aloud each day as thanks to God for daily bread. Sometime during the week enjoy bread and the psalm with another person. Let the taste, texture, and goodness of the bread remind you of the goodness of God.

20. Read Psalm 27 aloud daily—in daylight if possible. And each day follow the urging of verse 14: "Wait for the LORD." Sit silently, listening for God. Meditate on the safety, comfort, and guidance found in light.

21. Pray Psalm 116 aloud daily after reading the assigned Scriptures. Listen for different meanings in the psalm against the background of the day's Scripture.

22. Pray Psalm 80 aloud daily as a prayer for restoration of relationship with God. Think about what the community is asking of God and what the community is promising God in order for the relationship to be restored.

23. Locate art depicting the crucifixion of Jesus in books or on the internet. Choose a different image each day to accompany your praying Psalm 22 aloud. Or simply recall depictions you have seen of the Crucifixion as you pray the psalm.

24. Celebrate the Resurrection through praying Psalm 98 aloud daily. Work out some hand motions to express the joy of the psalm and use them as you pray.

25. As oil is God's blessing on worship and dew is God's blessing on creation in Psalm 133, unity is God's blessing on community in the letters of John and Jude. As you read Psalm 133 aloud daily, think of expressions of unity in the life of your congregation experienced as blessing. How would you symbolize those expressions of unity?

26. Keep your own speaking in mind as you pray Psalm 141 aloud daily. Focus on 141:3. Memorize it and repeat it to yourself throughout the day as you choose the words you say.

27. Follow each day's reading aloud of assigned Scripture with praying aloud Psalm 2. Think about how the psalm addresses each day's passages from Revelation.

28. Pray Psalm 86:1-11 aloud daily, knowing that God hears and wants to give the undivided heart necessary for the church to listen to what the Spirit is saying.

29. Combine reading Psalm 97 and writing a litany. Each day read the psalm aloud and write one sentence describing God, followed by *The LORD is king! Let the earth rejoice.* On the sixth day read the whole litany aloud after the psalm.

30. As you pray Psalm 26 aloud daily, reflect on the struggle of Christians and the church to remain faithful to God while surrounded by evil.

31. Each day pray Psalm 148 in the midst of creation. Read it aloud under the moon and stars, in the bright sunlight, surrounded by hills and mountains, with ocean in view, in falling rain or snow, in the hearing of young people and old, with birds and animals in sight. Call on all created things to praise God.

32. Pray Psalm 96 aloud daily. Choose a different recording of instrumental music to accompany your reading of the psalm each day. If you are able, consider praying the psalm on your knees.

The Radical Disciple

"The Radical Disciple" statements arise from each week's Scripture. They require stretch in terms of commitment, and they present challenge in terms of discipleship. The statements vary in intention and in the action called for—sometimes reflection and self-assessment, sometimes quiet affirmation in daily living, sometimes choosing an action or a direction that will be unsettling to self and others. Many of the challenges presented here will put disciples at odds with their culture and therefore cannot be undertaken lightly.

These descriptions of radical discipleship are not to be seen as exercises to be completed in a week— though some actions called for, such as writing a psalm, can be completed during a week. Rather, the challenge is life-changing and lifelong. DISCIPLE participants will choose to accept the challenge in some statements and not in others. Those who accept the challenges to radical discipleship will do so expecting support of a loving community of committed disciples. That's your challenge and your challenge to the group.

1. What family matters need your attention? Is there addictive behavior? Abuse? Failure to communicate? Need for reconciliation? Secrets that should be confronted? Financial problems? Isolation and loneliness? What would be the cost in time, energy, money?

2. The radical disciple recognizes that a name always brings with it a heritage and a heritage always makes claims. To take the name *Christian* is to accept the heritage and the demands behind the name. To take the name *disciple* is to accept the requirements that go with the name. The radical disciple intentionally lives up to the name.

3. Recognizing the human tendency to self-seeking that so often undermines the desire to seek God, the radical disciple practices prayer and repentance as disciplines of faithfulness—not once but continually.

4. Assuming the radical disciple is one who is at the direction of God in a way that is unusual, who is the radical disciple in this week's Scripture? If Cyrus, what is radical? If the returning exiles? If Ezra? If Nehemiah? If Darius or Artaxerxes? Consider the various persons and their actions. What about you? What unusual call is yours at the direction of God?

5. The radical disciple confronts in self and others attitudes and language that stereotype any group and cause or allow persecution to continue.

6. The radical disciple actively resists faith-denying elements in the culture. List the values most important to you, the principles that align you with God's kingdom. During the coming week, try to spot discrepancies between your values and your behavior.

7. The radical disciple, open to wisdom's guidance and correction, practices both discernment and discipline: *Discernment* in choosing the right path to wisdom and deciding which teachings apply in a given situation. *Discipline* in staying on the path and in making decisions informed by wisdom along the way.

8. The radical disciple goes beyond "being good" for reward to living rightly regardless of reward. What are you doing that requires passion, vision, hard work, proverbial wisdom, sacrificial love?

9. Enter into the spirit of the Teacher and identify those things over which you have no control. Relax in faith. Seek contentment rather than excess. Listen more than you speak. Find meaning in giving rather than getting. Let go the need to have final answers. Trust God.

10. Start the day with a prayer of thanksgiving. During the day, avoid complaining; express thanks to others. Reflect satisfaction in work done, help given and received. Be a friend. End the day with a prayer of gratitude and trust. Know that each day is a gift.

11. We prefer the cycle of *we believe, God blesses, we give thanks*. But tragedy comes. The radical disciple resists the urge to give pat answers. But more, the radical disciple goes to those who have lost their money, had their house burn down, or lost a family member to death and offers help and love in the name of Jesus. Most of all, the radical disciple practices the ministry of presence.

12. The radical disciple accepts life for what it is— a mixture of order *and* chaos, joy *and* despair, good *and* bad, reason *and* mystery—and lives trusting in God's purpose.

13. Risking vulnerability in loving and being loved, in knowing and being known, the radical disciple practices lavish self-giving and joyfully receives the self-giving of another. How are you doing?

14. The radical disciple dares to own all the psalms, including the unfamiliar and those deliberately avoided. Memorize a psalm or a portion of a psalm that expresses emotions you consider negative so that when you need those words you have them.

15. The radical disciple learns to express the full range of emotions to God. Write a personal lament. Base it on a past or present trouble. Include these elements: a call, description of the trouble, plea for God to respond, statement of trust that God is listening, a vow or expression of praise.

16. The radical disciple praises God. Write your own psalm of thanksgiving. Use Psalm 103 as your model. You may want to name God's victories and blessings in your life.

17. The radical disciple lives in a pluralistic society and at the same time believes that Jesus is the unique Word of God.

18. The radical disciple bears witness to the new life in Christ through daily acts of faithful living. How do you think your experience of new life is evident to those around you?

19. The radical disciple hears the hard sayings of Jesus and does not turn away. What teachings of Jesus in this week's Scripture did you find difficult?

20. Having seen the light of Christ, the radical disciple becomes a bearer of that light. Each day this week, decide where, how, and to whom you will take the light of Christ.

21. "Unless a grain of wheat falls into the earth and dies, it remains just a single grain; but if it dies, it bears much fruit" (John 12:24). What must the radical disciple die to, let go of, in life in order to bear fruit?

22. Describe what for you would be an act of servanthood. Pray during the week for the enabling power of the Holy Spirit. Then act.

23. In our society the cross is displayed as a decorative accessory as often as a sacred symbol. Watch for crosses displayed in various ways during the coming week. What message did each cross convey to you?

24. The radical disciple risks taking the good news of the empty tomb where others hesitate to go. Where is that for you?

25. When faced with new situations that call old assumptions, old commandments into question, the radical disciple views the situation with a clear eye, knows the limits of tolerance for change, and holds self and community to the central teaching of Christ.

26. During the coming week, listen. Listen for talk that tears down, belittles, degrades, undercuts—on radio and television and in movies; in conversations at home, at work, at play. Examine your own participation in such talk. Listen for positive uses of the tongue. Consider the relationship between your faith and your speech.

27. While society in general thinks culture—behavior patterns, beliefs, arts, entertainment, products—is benign, the radical disciple resists the power of everyday culture, knowing it undermines the sovereignty of God.

28. The radical disciple leads the way in calling the congregation to accountability and Christ-like faithfulness when the pull toward accommodation and compromise is strong.

29. The saints are praying continually; their prayers rise like incense. Perseverance makes praying radical. How might you become a more powerful person of prayer?

30. The radical disciple is willing to accept suffering but also knows how to give encouragement to others who are paying a price for their faith. Who needs your support?

31. The radical disciple acknowledges the reality of evil and calls it what it is, sees evil and confronts it, decides what action is necessary in the face of evil and proceeds with active hope.

Marks of Faithful Community

Each DISCIPLE *lesson identifies a particular mark of faithful community. All thirty-two marks are listed here.*

1. Being faithful community, we take family seriously, giving high priority to family responsibilities, even extended family, often at considerable sacrifice. We reach outside family to include others.

2. Being faithful community, we value the power of memory and heritage to form us into God's worshiping people, obedient in the present and responsible to the future.

3. Being faithful community, we freely choose to be bound together as the people of God.

4. Being faithful community, we stand ready to hear rather than not hear, ready to do rather than not do in order to respond to God's call and direction.

5. Being faithful community, we act in God's name when God seems silent. We stand up to persecution on God's behalf—whatever the form, wherever it occurs.

6. Being faithful community, we actively resist faith-denying elements in our culture, whatever the cost.

7. Being faithful community, we listen to wisdom and try to incorporate those insights into daily behavior.

8. Being faithful community, we trust God's wisdom, not the world's wisdom, in making our choices.

9. Being faithful community, we accept life's mystery in all of its forms, and we accept death as a part of life.

10. Being faithful community, we receive life as a gift, live it now, enjoy it, and thank God for it.

11. Being faithful community, we recognize the need to ask why when we experience suffering and injustice, and are assured of God's presence even when answers do not come.

12. Being faithful community, we approach God with a sense of awe, accepting God's sovereignty, acknowledging life's mystery, and rejoicing in our place in God's creation.

13. Being faithful community, we express and respond to the need and desire for intimacy by imitating God's lavish self-giving to us.

14. Being faithful community, we pray, knowing God welcomes us and knowing nothing we say or feel is outside that welcome.

15. Being faithful community, we take God's Word with us into pain and trouble and let the psalms of lament be our voice.

16. Being faithful community, we praise God because God is worthy of praise, whatever our life situation.

17. Being faithful community, we receive and claim the teaching of the community that Jesus is God in the flesh.

18. Being faithful community, we see life as both physical and spiritual, and while we exist in the physical, we live in new life graciously offered by God in Jesus Christ.

19. Being faithful community, we seek nothing less than "the food that endures for eternal life," Jesus the living bread.

20. Being faithful community, we choose to be diligent witnesses to the light of Christ.

21. Being faithful community, we live and die believing Jesus is the Messiah, the Son of God.

22. Being faithful community, we abide in Christ in order to bear the fruit of service.

23. Being faithful community, we receive with gratitude the selfless love of God in Christ shown on the cross and proclaim it in our living.

24. Being faithful community, we believe in the resurrected Christ and witness boldly to that victory with joy.

25. Being faithful community, we are shaped in our relationship to one another by the message we have heard from the beginning: Love one another.

26. Being faithful community, we recognize words have power to build up or destroy. Therefore, we do not take lightly the use of our tongue.

27. Being faithful community, we live and work in the present, expecting God's victory in the future, secure in knowing the end—whenever it comes—is in God's hands.

28. Being faithful community, we listen to what the Spirit of God is saying to our congregation and strive to be faithful.

29. Being faithful community, we refuse to be defined and confined by the routine; we take our place in the universal struggle, knowing that victory is assured.

30. Being faithful community, we choose to be faithful rather than fearful, bold in our witness whatever the cost.

31. Being faithful community, we live fully in the present, confronting the evil that surrounds us, and fully in the promise of God's new heaven and new earth.

32. Being faithful community, we rest in the knowledge that God is in control; we yield our lives in obedience to a God who stooped to wash feet and calls us to do the same for others.

Tending to Details

MARKING YOUR BIBLE

Start UNDER THE TREE OF LIFE study with a fresh, unmarked Bible so you approach the Scripture anew without influence of earlier notations and markings.

Mark your Bible to turn it into a personalized study Bible.

- Know why you are marking particular material.
- You may want to mark words or phrases that give you clues to the writer's message, names of people and places, sequence in the action, verses that have special meaning for you.
- Resist the temptation to mark the familiar simply because it is familiar.
- Indicate new insights or points about which you have questions.
- Identify passages to memorize.

Encourage other DISCIPLE group members to mark their Bibles as they read the daily assignments.

RESOURCES FOR TEACHING

These resources are suggested especially for the teacher, but group members would also find them useful.

Eerdmans Dictionary of the Bible, edited by David Noel Freedman (Wm. B. Eerdmans Publishing Co., 2000).

Tanakh: The Holy Scriptures (Jewish Publication Society, 1985).

The Message: The Old Testament Wisdom Books in Contemporary Language, by Eugene H. Peterson (NavPress Publishing Group, 1996).

The Wisdom Literature (Interpreting Biblical Texts Series), by Richard J. Clifford (Abingdon Press, 1998).

In the House of the Lord: Inhabiting the Psalms of Lament, by Michael Jinkins (Liturgical Press, 1998).

The Gospel and Letters of John (Interpreting Biblical Texts Series), by R. Alan Culpepper (Abingdon Press, 1998).

Revelation (Westminster Bible Companion Series), by Catherine Gunsalus González and Justo L. González (Westminster John Knox Press, 1997).

MEETING LOCATION AND EQUIPMENT

Consider the following factors in choosing and preparing a place for the weekly group meetings:
- physical accessibility to all group members;
- private enough to ensure no interruptions;
- adequate space for sitting or standing in groups for study activities;
- appropriate furniture, including tables large enough for spreading out books and for writing;
- availability of childcare;
- appropriate heating and cooling;
- video equipment in good working order, placed for easy viewing;
- chalkboard or newsprint pad.
- Sessions 31 and 32 require special room arrangements. See teacher helps pages 60–63 and related pages.

SOCIAL OCCASIONS

Fellowship, trust, and caring will deepen as persons get to know one another at times and in situations other than the weekly group meeting.
- Plan occasions when members invite spouses, other family members, and friends for a time of relaxed visiting, playing, and eating together.
- You may want to celebrate holidays or days or events that are special to members of the group.
- The point of such gatherings is to have leisure time together. Keep the occasions informal and fairly simple.

SERVICE OF RECOGNITION

Completion of study of DISCIPLE: UNDER THE TREE OF LIFE by groups of twelve and their teacher is cause for recognition, celebration, and thanksgiving by the whole congregation. Plan such an occasion as a part of a morning or evening worship service.
- Invite a member of the governing body of the congregation to express the gratitude of the congregation to those who have studied and prepared themselves for faithful ministry in and through the congregation.
- Invite group members to describe what the study experience meant to them.
- Include prayer for members of the congregation who will form similar groups of twelve for study.
- Present certificates of recognition and pins to persons who have completed UNDER THE TREE OF LIFE.
- Present the special multiphase pin to persons who have completed all four DISCIPLE studies. (This pin must be special-ordered.)

Preparing to Teach DISCIPLE

- Prepare as a participant in the group, a learner among learners, as well as the teacher of the group.

- Do not rely on your familiarity with Scripture or on study done previously. Come to each lesson and its daily assignments as a beginner, as though you were reading the Scripture passages for the first time.

- Expect weekly preparation by group members and plan the group meeting process on that basis.

- Your role in the group meeting will be mainly in keeping the process going rather than in being the giver of information. No doubt, members of the group will look to you for some new or additional information, but don't let them put you into the position of being the authority or the expert. Regularly change where you sit in the group to avoid authority being given to one person in one place.

- Pay attention to the amount of time available for covering the main parts of the work to be done in each group meeting: use of the video segment, review and discussion of the weekly assignment, group study of a passage of Scripture, and commitment to ministry.

- Plan activities that will allow a balance among work done in the total group, work done in small groups or pairs, and work done as individuals. Choice of activity or teaching approach will vary according to the particular Scripture being studied.

- Your own reading of the assigned Scripture and the study manual will suggest to you ways of reviewing and making use of the material in the group meeting.

- Decide a sequence and process for handling the daily study notes persons have written. Here are some possibilities:
  1. Work through the sheet of notes and related Scriptures day by day, talking together in the total group, in small groups, or in pairs.
  2. Identify and list on newsprint all the questions persons had as they did their reading and study in preparation for the group meeting. Some of these questions will be answered by group members; others may require further study and discussion by the group.
  3. Work together to identify and organize the information gathered by group members in their study:
       Make time charts;
       develop glossaries of words;
       list key persons and events;
       identify and discuss biblical and theological ideas;
       establish the setting of the Scriptures being studied;
       make connections to other Scriptures and to life situations;
       discuss insights, experiences, feelings.
  4. Interpret the text in terms of the meaning originally intended.

- Anticipate the points where the group might get sidetracked or take a direction different from the one you have planned: the raising of an unanswerable question or a theological issue over which differences of opinion or debate are likely to occur. Be prepared to handle such occurrences.

- Include time in your plan for hearing reports from group members who have done additional study and research. If several persons have prepared reports on the same subject, vary the presentation through the use of a panel, by having one person give the report and others provide additional details, or form small groups for hearing the reports.

- Try to have some activity in each group meeting that has the group reading Scripture aloud or hearing the Scriptures read aloud.

- Plan an occasional activity that will require group members to use Bible commentaries, atlases, and dictionaries during the meeting to do further research for clarification or to locate additional information.

Group Building and Maintenance

The Climate for a Good Group

A good climate for study may be described in words such as these: *warmth, trust, enthusiasm, patience, open-mindedness, caring, acceptance, sensitivity, humor,* and *informality.*

In a healthy study climate, both the individual and the group are respected. Persons are attentive and sensitive to one another's thoughts and feelings, and persons feel comfortable in expressing honestly their deepest thoughts and feelings.

Drawing Out Quiet Persons

- Recognize that persons participate in ways other than talking and that a person has a right not to speak. Allow persons to pass rather than respond to a particular question or in a particular activity.
- Emphasize that all contributions have value. Hesitancy to speak may be related to a fear of saying the wrong thing or of appearing foolish.
- Be sensitive to when the quiet person may want to speak and simply needs some encouragement from the teacher. Watch for nonverbal clues. Take care not to embarrass by asking a direct question but rather by inviting a person to speak through such phrases as "You look as though you would like to add something."
- Plan small group discussion and activity, because those who are reluctant to participate in conversation in the larger group may feel comfortable doing so in a small group. Put groups together with care. Begin by putting the quieter persons together and the more dominant persons together. Gradually mix the groups so that persons will have opportunity to work with everyone.

Working With the Person Who Monopolizes

Tact and sensitivity are called for in responding to persons who tend to monopolize the conversation in the group.

- Be sensitive to what the persons are saying by their behavior as well as in their words.
- Recognize that your attitude toward the person who is dominating will be communicated through your tone of voice, body language, and facial expression as well as through your words.
- One response you may make is to summarize what the person has said and invite others to add to the discussion or to give their opinion.
- Lessen the opportunity for domination by a person or persons through the choice of group activities that employ small group work or team work or directed work that involves response from each person in turn.
- Rely on other group members to help manage the group process. When a group is functioning well, all persons in the group take some responsibility for participation and thereby cut down the possibility of one person dominating.

Group building and maintenance should be discussed when the study group is forming and deciding on ground rules. The ground rules might include some agreements about how persons are expected to participate and how the group will monitor itself.

Handling Conflicting Opinions in the Study Group

A healthy group climate depends on the understanding that differences of opinion are welcomed, that persons are encouraged to think for themselves, and that persons may feel comfortable in disagreeing with one another and with the teacher.

The teacher who is not personally threatened by views contrary to his or her own will quickly establish a tone of trust and acceptance in the group. When conflict of opinion occurs, treat it as good, natural, and potentially rewarding.

- Maintain responsibility for the direction of the session.
- Keep the exchange of ideas focused on the topic, not on the persons involved in the discussion.
- At appropriate points in the discussion, summarize the major points and identify the points of difference and agreement.
- Continually relate the discussion to the session topic.
- Turn the discussion into an occasion for further work by the group through use of Bible dictionaries, commentaries, and other such aids.
- Recognize that sometimes resolution is not desirable, necessary, or possible, and that continuing difference of opinion is acceptable.
- If the discusssion is not relevant to all group members, suggest that those who wish may talk further after the group has adjourned.
- Be aware of time and know when to move on with other work planned for the session.
- Compliment the group on the enthusiasm and strong feelings they bring to their discussion of such matters.
- Demonstrate caring and acceptance of persons both during and after points of conflict.

Preparing Questions and Leading Discussion

Group discussion that goes beyond the sharing of opinions or biases and superficial answers requires careful preparation by individual group members and by the teacher. Thinking that goes into productive discussion combines purpose and discipline.

PREPARING QUESTIONS

Be clear about what you want to accomplish through the questions you prepare.
- Questions can help persons think.
- Questions can open minds to new insights or knowledge.
- Questions can enable the examining of an idea, an understanding, an assumption.
- Questions often require probing deeper into a subject.

Different kinds of questions serve different purposes. Write questions with specific functions in mind.
- If your purpose is to gather or call to mind certain information, write questions that use recall, ask for facts, or require a specific correct answer.
- If your purpose is to organize data, write questions that ask persons to describe, compare, or contrast data.
- If your purpose is to analyze a situation or an action, write questions that call for explanation or reasons related to the situation or action.
- If your purpose is to make connections or draw conclusions, write questions that call for persons to summarize or state the relationship or connection among previously unrelated data.
- If your purpose is to have persons make judgments or evaluate, write questions that call for them to tell which choice is best according to specific criteria.
- If your purpose is to speculate about an outcome or a situation, write open-ended questions that allow for imagination and the identification of many possibilities.

Know what kind of question you are asking and indicate to the group the reason you are asking it.

When writing questions, keep these considerations in mind:
- Generally yes-and-no questions are too specific and tend to close off discussion.
- Questions are generally poor when their answer is too self-evident, when no answer is possible, when they are too involved, or when they are too vague.

- A good mixture of questions deals with information and with feelings and experiences.
- The best questions are stated simply and have only one focus.
- A good question generally takes persons back to earlier study and preparation and stimulates further inquiry.
- Key words for factual questions are *what, where, when, why, who,* and *how.*
- Before using the questions you have written to lead discussion, test the questions by trying to answer them yourself.

LEADING DISCUSSION

- State the question to be discussed. Help group members to know what they are discussing and why.

- Have in mind some idea of how the discussion ought to develop.

- Allow time for thought. Don't be afraid of silence, because silence need not be empty; and it invites thought. Don't rush to rephrase the question. If the question is well written, it will bring response eventually. Avoid answering your own questions, because persons will soon learn that you do and will depend on you to do so.

- Listen. Be sensitive to feelings as well as to words. Listening includes awareness of the speaker's point of view as well as the words being heard. Occasionally summarize what is being said without evaluating or judging.

- Indicate your listening by eye contact, a nod of the head, and a spoken word or two.

- Remember that you stop listening when you begin to think about how you are going to respond.

- Avoid approving or disapproving, agreeing or disagreeing (unless there is an error in fact) with what a person is saying.

- Acceptance of people does not require acceptance of their ideas, interpretations, attitudes.

- Create possibilities for all persons to contribute so that none monopolizes the discussion.

- Know where you are headed with the discussion so that as other questions arise you will not lose the direction you first set.

Principles for Bible Study

1 The Word of God is Jesus Christ, and the words of the Bible tell us about that Word. Therefore, when we study the words of the Bible we always look behind, in, and through those words for God's Word—Jesus Christ.

2 No Christian has a monopoly on understanding either God's Word or the words of the Scripture. This includes biblical scholars and the most unlearned Christian. All of us must listen to one another as we seek to understand the richness of God's gifts.

3 We must assume everyone has Christian integrity and not accuse one another of being unchristian, no matter how unusual are the opinions.

4 We must further assume that we will arrive at different understandings of portions of Scripture and that that will not disturb God as much as it will some of us.

5 Few of us will know Hebrew or Greek, and we therefore need to use a variety of English versions to try to understand the text.

6 While we accept our differences, we do not feel that those differences are unimportant, or that they should be ignored or treated as if they did not matter.

7 Different biblical understandings can remain among us, but we can still be warm Christian friends. In fact, as we grow to better understand our differences, we can grow in our appreciation of one another.

Orientation Meeting

When you have the full list of persons who have made the commitment to be a part of your DISCIPLE group, schedule a one-to-one-and-a-half-hour orientation meeting one week prior to the first weekly group meeting.

The purpose of the orientation meeting is
- to discuss and agree on a schedule for the nine-month study;
- to distribute the study manuals and become acquainted with elements in the lesson format;
- to understand the commitment being undertaken by members of the group;
- to begin building open, trusting relationships, because the group may be a mixture of persons from several DISCIPLE groups and, even though persons may have been together in an earlier DISCIPLE group, they are now different persons because all time brings change.

Explain the small-group process you will be using and emphasize that you are a learner among learners, not a lecturer or information giver, and that you will be an equal participant in the activities.

Describe the environment for study as one of openness and trust where every person's opinions will be valued.

Emphasize that as the study progresses and the discussion becomes more personal, confidentiality will be an important factor; and that if a situation arises when you cannot be present to lead a session, you will ask members of the group to lead the session, not someone from outside the group.

Emphasize that you will be paying close attention to time during the weekly meeting and that all parts of the group meeting format will be covered every week.

Stress that you will start the weekly group meeting on time and end on time.

Mention that the last two sessions will include extended worship experiences: Session 31 (3½ hours), a video-led experience of Revelation as worship (see handbook pages 13–14), and Session 32 (3½ to 4 hours), a love feast that includes footwashing.

Identify additional sources of information: Bible dictionaries, atlases, commentaries, and concordances. Let persons know if the church has such sources available and how they might borrow them.

Distribute during the meeting the thirty-two-week schedule, study manuals, handbooks, and "Principles for Bible Study," copied from the teacher helps.

Orientation Meeting Agenda

7:00 P.M. Prayer

7:05 P.M. Group member introductions

7:10 P.M. Verify the meeting calendar.
- Note longer Sessions 31 and 32.
- Discuss holiday breaks.
- Make necessary adjustments.

7:20 P.M. Distribute handbooks and read pages 6–7. Preview the study manual and how it will be used (see study manual page 4 and teacher helps page 4).
- Explain the need for a good study Bible.
- Emphasize daily notetaking.
- Call attention to the "Psalm of the Week."
- Explain the purpose and placement of "The Radical Disciple."

7:35 P.M. Review the weekly meeting schedule and format (see teacher helps page 5).
- Discuss related issues—meeting location, video setup, childcare arrangements, refreshment schedule.

7:55 P.M. Read "Principles for Bible Study" responsively.
- Highlight transformation as the key to DISCIPLE.

8:00 P.M. Preview Session 1.
- Highlight daily assignments.
- Establish a plan of mutual prayer support.
- Emphasize the importance of praying the "Psalm of the Week" aloud each day.

8:10 P.M. Explore study aids in the Bible that would be particularly useful for this study.
- Identify additional sources of information.

8:25 P.M. Closing Covenant
Reiterate the commitment required of DISCIPLE Bible study (see handbook pages 19 and 21).
Lead group in covenanting together to
- Pray daily for one another.
- Prepare daily by reading and taking notes.
- Be present every week but faithful to study when absent.
- Participate in every session by both listening and discussing.

8:30 P.M. Dismiss

Notes

DISCIPLE

THE WRITINGS

1 Redeem the Inheritance

GATHERING AND PRAYER

(5 minutes)

Begin on time with those who are there. Use the theme word, theme verse, title, "Our Human Condition," and prayer from the study manual.

VIDEO SEGMENT 1

(20 minutes)
Presenter: Amy-Jill Levine

Prepare to View Video

Pay attention to the location of Ruth in the Jewish and Christian canons and to the themes included in the Hebrew word *chesed* (*hesed*, HEH-sed).

View Video

Summary of video content:

Ruth is a narrative about often-difficult relationships and the means by which they are negotiated.

The Jewish canon places Ruth among the Writings or Kethuvim.

Chesed combines themes of lovingkindness and loyalty, redemption, and inclusion.

The book of Ruth places Obed in the line of Boaz. Ruth's story is seen as demonstrating providence.

Discuss After Viewing Video

What did you hear about the placement and purpose of the book of Ruth? What is *chesed*? How are lives transformed as a result of *chesed*? What questions about existence confront us in this text?

SCRIPTURE AND STUDY MANUAL

(50 minutes adults)   (35 minutes youth)

Study the daily Scriptures in three ways.

(1) Assign each person one or more of these passages: Judges 3:12-30; Leviticus 19; 23:9-22; Deuteronomy 24:10-22; 25:5-10; Genesis 38; Jeremiah 32:1-15; 1 Chronicles 2:1-17; Matthew 1:1-17. Review each with these questions in mind: What does this passage contribute to the setting or environment in which Ruth's story unfolds? to the power in the story? Hear what each person discovers.

(2) In groups of four use daily notes on Ruth 1–4 to answer these questions: Where is *chesed* (lovingkindness) at work in relationships in this story? Where are human beings carrying out God's providential care? Hear written responses to the questions on study manual page 10 and top of page 13.

(3) Look at psalms of deliverance and thanksgiving through Ruth's story. Make these assignments: Group 1—Psalms 13; 77; 103; Group 2—Psalms 69 and 111. How might these words have spoken for the characters and about situations in Ruth?

BREAK

(10 minutes)

ENCOUNTER THE WORD

(40 minutes adults)   (20 minutes youth)

Scripture selection: Ruth 4

Read the passage silently. Establish the setting, who is there, what is going on. Ask persons to close their eyes and imagine themselves as Boaz. What is he thinking? What is he feeling? But give no answers. Follow the same procedure for the next-of-kin, the elders, the women, Naomi. Discuss these questions in pairs or threes: What insights did you get into the people and the passage? What did you feel in each role? Then reread Ruth 4 as dialogue in the total group. (See mental drama, pages 102–4 of *Teaching the Bible to Adults and Youth*, by Dick Murray.)

MARKS OF FAITHFUL COMMUNITY

(20 minutes)

Being faithful community, we take family seriously, giving high priority to family responsibilities, even extended family, often at considerable sacrifice. We reach outside family to include others.

Read aloud "Our Human Condition" and the mark of faithful community. Describe characteristics of faithful community. Which ones move persons from the situation in "Our Human Condition" to the situation in "Marks of Faithful Community"? In pairs or threes discuss written responses to the first four questions under "Marks of Faithful Community," study manual pages 13–14. Then in two groups discuss the last two items in this section.

"The Radical Disciple": In pairs reflect silently on the questions under this heading. Say what the term *radical disciple* means. What is being called for by these questions that would be radical for you?

CLOSING AND PRAYER

(5 minutes adults)   (10 minutes youth)

Check Lesson 2 assignments. Hear prayer concerns. Close by reading Psalm 146 responsively.

2 The Dream Restored

GATHERING AND PRAYER

(5 minutes)

VIDEO SEGMENT 2

(25 minutes)
Presenter: Leslie C. Allen

Prepare to View Video

Listen for the Chronicler's answers to his question, How do we get full restoration from exile?

View Video

Summary of video content:

Genealogy in 1 Chronicles 1–9 stresses the people's identity as twelve tribes, places the tribe of Levi in the middle of the account as a symbol of the central role of the Temple, gives special importance to the line of David.

First Chronicles 10 through Second Chronicles develops three themes: communal inclusivity, the Temple, and the role of the Davidic dynasty.

Discuss After Viewing Video

In the Chronicler's view, what would the genealogies, the Temple, and the Davidic dynasty contribute to the restoration of the people after exile?

SCRIPTURE AND STUDY MANUAL

(50 minutes adults)   (35 minutes youth)

To get a sense of the importance of genealogies to restoration of a people, in groups of three review 1 Chronicles 1–9 and daily notes to answer these questions: What kind of information is here other than family names? Why would these lists have been important to returned exiles?

The Chronicler's theological emphasis is expressed and supported through certain persons or agencies: David, Solomon, Temple, Jerusalem, tribe of Judah, Israel, Levites. In groups of four or six use assigned Scripture and daily notes to recall the theological significance the Chronicler attached to each. Then discuss this question in the total group: How might the Chronicler's emphasis on theology inspire Israel to become an obedient people?

David and the kingdom symbolize the bond between God and Israel, centered in the Temple. Study Scripture to get a picture of that bond. First read aloud 1 Samuel 16:1-13 and 1 Chronicles 10:13–11:9. Form pairs and assign one passage to each pair: 1 Chronicles 13; 15–16; 17; 21:1–22:1; 22:2-19; 24–26; 28–29. Instruct the pairs to get in mind the main points in their passage. Allow time for study. Then tell the story in sequence with each pair contributing. Discuss this question: What do you see and hear in these stories that symbolizes the bond between God and Israel?

Pray Psalm 132 aloud and invite brief remembrances of persons who passed on both a place and a heritage of faith.

BREAK

(10 minutes)

ENCOUNTER THE WORD

(35 minutes adults)   (15 minutes youth)
Scripture selection: 1 Chronicles 14
Read 1 Chronicles 14 silently. Work in pairs on these questions: What does the passage actually say? What did the passage likely mean to its first hearers? What do you think the Chronicler intended to convey in this account? Reread the passage and continue discussion. What elements are the same or different in the situation in David's time and in the twenty-first century? What meaning does the passage have for today? (See depth Bible study, pages 35–39 of *Teaching the Bible to Adults and Youth*.)

MARKS OF FAITHFUL COMMUNITY

(20 minutes)

Being faithful community, we value the power of memory and heritage to form us into God's worshiping people, obedient in the present and responsible to the future.

Read "Our Human Condition" and the mark of faithful community aloud. Discuss these questions: What criteria are we to use as we decide what to value from the past and from the present? Read "Our Human Condition" again. Then consider "The Radical Disciple." What heritage and what demands come with the names *Christian* and *disciple?*

Respond in pairs or threes to the five questions under "Marks of Faithful Community."

CLOSING AND PRAYER

(5 minutes adults)   (10 minutes youth)
Turn to Lesson 3 and check assignments. Write down prayer concerns. Close with prayer.

3 Rise and Fall of Faithfulness

GATHERING AND PRAYER

(5 minutes)

VIDEO SEGMENT 3

(20 minutes)
Presenter: Cheryl B. Anderson

Prepare to View Video

Listen for the connection the Chronicler makes between faithfulness to God and Temple worship in Jerusalem, and for the role of priests and Levites.

View Video

Summary of video content:

The Chronicler covers only the history of Judah.

The Chronicler underscores the significance of Jerusalem and Temple worship.

Priests and Levites were Temple officials responsible for upholding the religious traditions.

Discuss After Viewing Video

From the Chronicler's perspective what constituted faithfulness to God? Why did the Chronicler focus his attention on the Southern Kingdom of Judah? What roles did priests and Levites play?

SCRIPTURE AND STUDY MANUAL

(50 minutes adults)   (35 minutes youth)

Form two groups to prepare and present aspects of Solomon and his reign. In both groups scan 2 Chronicles 1–9 and daily notes to identify points to emphasize. The presentation might be a pantomime, poem, song, litany, rap, minidrama, or synopsis. Allow several minutes for groups to prepare their presentation. Instruct groups to end their portrayal by reading aloud a Scripture passage: Group 1—1 Kings 11:41-43; Group 2—2 Chronicles 9:29-31.

To fill out the picture of Solomon, read 1 Kings 11:1-40 aloud. Identify causes of deterioration that led eventually to division of the kingdom. In pairs or threes review the reigns of Rehoboam and Jeroboam in 2 Chronicles 10–13. Why does the story say God divided the kingdom?

The Chronicler's account of the kings of Judah (2 Chronicles 14–36, Days 3–5) is a record of the conflict between true worship and abandonment of faith. In groups of three or four work through the chapters, naming each king and watching for recurring words and phrases that signal obedience or failure

and deterioration. What actions and attitudes lead to sin and failure? What actions and attitudes demonstrate obedience? What are the roots of apostasy? of true worship? Where is the Chronicler's theology of cause and effect being made clear in this history of the Davidic kings? Respond to the questions on study manual page 29 and top of page 31.

BREAK

(10 minutes)

ENCOUNTER THE WORD

(40 minutes adults)   (20 minutes youth)

Scripture selection: 2 Chronicles 7:12-22

Hear 2 Chronicles 7:12-22 read aloud. In groups of three or four study the passage using these questions: What does the passage tell us about God? What does it tell us about human beings? What does it tell us about the relationship between God and human beings? Then respond to this question: What clues do you get from this passage about the Chronicler's theology? State the Chronicler's theology in a sentence. Hear each group's sentence. (See theological Bible study, pages 40–44 of *Teaching the Bible to Adults and Youth*.)

MARKS OF FAITHFUL COMMUNITY

(20 minutes)

Being faithful community, we freely choose to be bound together as the people of God.

Read "Our Human Condition" silently and think about Solomon. How are his weaknesses mirrored here? Talk in groups of three or four. What parts of "Our Human Condition" does the mark of faithful community call into question? Now discuss the first question under "Marks of Faithful Community," study manual page 31. Next read 2 Chronicles 7:14, study manual page 24, and "The Radical Disciple." What new insights do they provide on leadership? How does your congregation's worship regularly encourage and support the discipline of prayer and repentance? Discuss the remaining two questions.

CLOSING AND PRAYER

(5 minutes adults)   (10 minutes youth)

Turn to Lesson 4 and check assignments. Write down prayer concerns. Pray Psalm 85 aloud.

4 To Build Again

GATHERING AND PRAYER

(5 minutes)

Before the Video

Last week's Scripture ended with Judah going into exile. Pause to mourn with Judah before beginning this week's return from exile. Allow time for everyone to choose a verse from Lamentations 2–5 to read later as a lament. Then hear Lamentations 1 read aloud, followed by each person's verse of lament. Finally, read together Ezra 1:2-3, study manual page 32.

VIDEO SEGMENT 4

(25 minutes)
Presenter: Jin Hee Han

Prepare to View Video

Note participants and events involved in restoration of a people and their religious community. Listen for these words: *Temple, Torah, town.*

View Video
Summary of video content:

In 538 B.C.E. Cyrus permitted the Jewish people to return to Jerusalem and rebuild their sanctuary.

Temple restoration had opposition.

Ezra initiated reform aimed at giving a sense of identity based on Torah.

Nehemiah repaired the wall and rebuilt the city.

The one constant presence: the God of Israel.

Discuss After Viewing Video

Where did you detect the presence of God active in people and events to bring about restoration? What did the *Temple, Torah,* and *town* contribute to restoration of a people?

SCRIPTURE AND STUDY MANUAL

(50 minutes adults)   (35 minutes youth)

The week's assignment urged reading Scripture for theological meaning rather than for historical detail. In two groups review the week's Scripture and daily notes, looking for examples of dependence on God expressed in actions, words, prayers, confessions, and the people's conviction they were responding to God's direction. Group 1—Ezra 1–10 and Haggai 1–2; Group 2—Nehemiah 1–13.

Consider people in this week's Scripture who characterize the radical disciple. Read "The Radical Disciple." In groups of three or four discuss what it means to be "at the direction of God in a way that is unusual." Then respond to the questions under "The Radical Disciple."

In the total group recall Ezra's agony over the problem of mixed marriages. Describe what was at issue for Ezra and the religious community. Respond to the question at the top of study manual page 39.

Pray Psalm 126 aloud and invite persons to say how they expressed its sense of joy as they read it daily. Sing "Bringing In the Sheaves."

BREAK

(10 minutes)

ENCOUNTER THE WORD

(35 minutes adults)   (15 minutes youth)
Scripture selection: Haggai 1

Hear Haggai 1 read aloud and then instruct the group to read the passage again silently using these questions as a guide: What docs the passage say? What happened? What did the writer intend to communicate? What did the situation likely mean to those who were present? Respond to the questions in pairs or threes. Reread the passage and respond to these questions: As twenty-first-century people what do we say to the passage? How does God address us in this passage? What claim does this passage make on me? (See dialogue and encounter, pages 51–56 of *Teaching the Bible to Adults and Youth*.)

MARKS OF FAITHFUL COMMUNITY

(20 minutes)

Being faithful community, we stand ready to hear rather than not hear, ready to do rather than not do in order to respond to God's call and direction.

In groups of three respond one at a time to the first instruction under "Marks of Faithful Community." Then read "Our Human Condition" and respond to the first question in this section. Now read the mark of faithful community and respond to the second and third questions.

CLOSING AND PRAYER

(5 minutes adults)   (10 minutes youth)

Check Lesson 5 assignments. Note need for Apocrypha. Hear prayer concerns. Close with prayer.

5 For Such a Time As This

GATHERING AND PRAYER

(5 minutes)

VIDEO SEGMENT 5

(25 minutes)
Presenter: Sidnie White Crawford

Prepare to View Video

Be aware of Esther's evolving role and the importance of banquets and role reversal to the plot.

View Video

Summary of video content:
Esther is the festival legend for the Feast of Purim.
Mordecai and Esther are Diaspora Jews.
Esther conceals her Jewish identity.
Haman and Mordecai are hereditary enemies.
The casting of Pur becomes the origin of Purim.

Discuss After Viewing Video

How does Esther operate? At what points did you see Esther growing into her role? How do banquets and role reversal function in the story?

SCRIPTURE AND STUDY MANUAL

(50 minutes adults)   (35 minutes youth)
Look at the Esther story from different perspectives. Form three groups to review Scripture for Days 1–3 with a particular purpose in mind: Group 1—Identify all the things that had to happen for the story to work. Group 2—What elements are necessary to the development of each of the characters—Ahasuerus, Vashti, Mordecai, Esther, eunuchs, Haman, Zeresh? What does each character contribute to the story? Group 3—What elements in the setting are necessary to the story? How does the setting function in the story? Work in groups for ten to twelve minutes and then hear from each group.

Compare the familiar book of Esther with the Greek version found in the Apocrypha. In groups of four or six examine Scripture and notes for Days 4–5 and recall Scripture for Days 1–3. Discuss these questions: What differences between the two versions did you see in the story, in the personalities and actions of the characters, in the purpose of the two authors? In your view, which account is more powerful? Say why.

Now discuss the two questions at the end of the first paragraph on study manual page 45. Invite the group to read aloud the quotation beginning "Not one only . . . " Reflect on the quotation and respond individually with words of lament.

BREAK

(10 minutes)

ENCOUNTER THE WORD

(35 minutes adults)   (15 minutes youth)
Scripture selection: Esther 3
Hear Esther 3 read aloud. For context, recall the history that ties Mordecai and Haman together. In groups of three or four study the passage using these questions: What does the passage say? What happened? What does the writer intend to say? Allow ten minutes for discussion. Reread the passage silently and discuss these questions: What do I say to the passage? As twenty-first-century people, what do we say to this passage? What does God say to me in this passage? How am I involved in this situation? What claim does this passage place on me? (See dialogue and encounter, pages 51–56 of *Teaching the Bible to Adults and Youth*.)

MARKS OF FAITHFUL COMMUNITY

(20 minutes)
Being faithful community, we act in God's name when God seems silent. We stand up to persecution on God's behalf—whatever the form, wherever it occurs.

Read "Our Human Condition" aloud. Reflect for a moment: What response do you think Vashti, Mordecai, or Esther would have made to this statement? Talk about it. Read the mark of faithful community. How does it challenge "Our Human Condition"? In pairs or threes respond to the questions under "Marks of Faithful Community." Now look at the mark of faithful community and "The Radical Disciple" together. Read aloud Esther 3:8. How have you heard these sentiments voiced? What response did you make? Think about other groups. What stands must we take on God's behalf?

CLOSING AND PRAYER

(5 minutes adults)   (10 minutes youth)
Turn to Lesson 6 and check assignments. Write down prayer concerns. Pray Psalm 83 aloud and close with a prayer for Israel and its neighbors.

6 The Approaching Kingdom

GATHERING AND PRAYER

(5 minutes)

VIDEO SEGMENT 6

(20 minutes)
Presenter: David A. deSilva

Prepare to View Video

Listen to a discussion of what kind of book Daniel is and how it has been used and applied.

View Video

Summary of video content:

Christians place Daniel among the Prophets; Jews place Daniel in the Writings.

"Prophetic" reading represents a stage in the reinterpretation and application of those texts to new situations.

The prophecies of Daniel have the form of prediction but are really looking back at the events they describe.

Discuss After Viewing Video

What kind of book is Daniel? How has it been understood, used, and applied? What is the purpose of the stories? What is the purpose of the visions?

SCRIPTURE AND STUDY MANUAL

(50 minutes adults)　　(35 minutes youth)

To get some sense of how the God of Daniel came to be regarded in Babylon, look at Scripture through the lens of Daniel 6:26-27. Read Daniel 6:26-27 aloud from study manual page 46. Then in groups of three or four consider Scripture passages for Days 1–2 one at a time with this question in mind: How does this Scripture illustrate or bear out the truth of Daniel 6:26-27? Ask both about what happened and its meaning.

To make the connection between the Daniel stories and life today, respond in pairs or threes to the questions on study manual page 49 one at a time. After some discussion look at "Our Human Condition," study manual page 46. What connection do you see between the situations in the questions just discussed and "Our Human Condition"?

Sort out the visions. What do the visions offer the reader in terms of symbols or images, history, geography, descriptions of earthly kingdoms, the approach of the kingdom of God, and Antiochus

IV? Work in two groups to draw information from Scripture and notes for Day 3 and study manual pages 51–53. See annotations in Bibles also.

Daniel and Second Esdras are apocalypses. Apocalyptic literature is characterized by a negative view of this world, hope for salvation in a new creation or another life, and encouragement for the faithful. In groups of three or four identify some of these characteristics in 2 Esdras 3:1–5:20 and recall any from the book of Daniel.

BREAK

(10 minutes)

ENCOUNTER THE WORD

(40 minutes adults)　　(20 minutes youth)

Scripture selection: Daniel 3:1-18

Write a modern version of the story set in our country, in our day. First be clear about the story. Hear the Scripture read aloud. In groups of three or four discuss these questions: What persons or entities are involved in the story? What are their roles? What is being called for and why? What equipped the young men to make their response? Reread the Scripture silently. Next, update the story: What form does the call take today? Who or what are the actors in the modern story? What are realistic substitute symbols, actions, consequences? What response may be expected from modern-day persons? Now create a modern version of the story. Hear the modern versions in the total group.

MARKS OF FAITHFUL COMMUNITY

(20 minutes)

Being faithful community, we actively resist faith-denying elements in our culture, whatever the cost.

Discuss the first question on study manual page 53. Read "Our Human Condition" and the mark of faithful community. Talk together about the tension between these two statements. Hear persons say what they discovered about themselves in following "The Radical Disciple" suggestion. Then discuss responses to the last two questions in this section.

CLOSING AND PRAYER

(5 minutes adults)　　(10 minutes youth)

Turn to Lesson 7 and check assignments. Write down prayer concerns. Close by praying Psalm 9.

7 The Beginning of Knowledge

GATHERING AND PRAYER

(5 minutes)

VIDEO SEGMENT 7

(20 minutes)
Presenter: Raymond C. Van Leeuwen

Prepare to View Video

Listen for three themes—the characteristics of Israel's wisdom, the concept of "the fear of the Lord," and the contrast between wisdom and folly.

View Video

Summary of video content:

Israel's wisdom included the fear of the Lord, insight into basic life patterns, ability to apply that insight, ability to act on insight.

"The fear of the Lord" is shorthand for all of life lived in devotion to God.

Life is a journey of two ways—the way of folly, the way of wisdom.

Discuss After Viewing Video

How did Israel's wisdom differ from the wisdom of Israel's neighbors? What does "the fear of the Lord" mean, and how does it influence wise living? Describe the way of folly and the way of wisdom.

SCRIPTURE AND STUDY MANUAL

(50 minutes adults)   (35 minutes youth)

Pray Psalm 1 aloud. Invite persons to read their rewrite of the psalm substituting other images for *trees* and *chaff*.

Proverbs 1:7 and "Our Human Condition," study manual page 54, provide context for beginning discussion of wisdom. Read the proverb and then "Our Human Condition" aloud in unison. Reverse the sequence and read them aloud again. Talk in pairs about what you heard when the proverb and statement were read together.

Consider some study manual statements about wisdom and folly: "Wisdom is the way things really are." "Wisdom contains the character of God in the stuff of existence." "Folly represents invitation to evil in general." "Choices have consequences." In groups of four or six consider the statements one at a time. Say what you think the statement is saying, what it means. Give an illustration or an example. In terms of your own knowledge and experience,

where do you see truth in each of the statements?

To get an overview of the counsel contained in Proverbs 1–15, form pairs or threes and assign one day's Scripture to each group. Instruct groups to look for Proverbs with any of these themes—emphasis on moral formation, contrasts between the wicked and the righteous, the way of wisdom and the way of folly, fear of God as the beginning of wisdom, and relationship between choice and consequence. Allow about ten minutes for working with Scripture. Then hear what persons have discovered.

BREAK

(10 minutes)

ENCOUNTER THE WORD

(40 minutes adults)   (20 minutes youth)

Scripture selection: Proverbs 3:1-12; 3:21-35

Hear the passages read aloud. Form two groups to paraphrase the passages. Assign one passage to a group. In the two groups talk through the assigned passage verse by verse to determine what is being said and how it might be said differently. Each group will create one paraphrase. Hear the paraphrases. (See paraphrasing, pages 71–76 of *Teaching the Bible to Adults and Youth*.)

MARKS OF FAITHFUL COMMUNITY

(20 minutes)

Being faithful community, we listen to wisdom and try to incorporate those insights into daily behavior.

In groups of three or four respond to the three questions under "Marks of Faithful Community." Then read the mark of faithful community. Discuss this question: To what extent and in what ways does the conviction underlying the mark of faithful community erase the feelings expressed in "Our Human Condition"? Read the description of "The Radical Disciple." What is taken account of in choosing the right path to wisdom and deciding which teachings apply in a given situation? What side roads, bumps, dead ends complicate staying on wisdom's path?

CLOSING AND PRAYER

(5 minutes adults)   (10 minutes youth)

Turn to Lesson 8 and check assignments. Write down prayer concerns. Close with a song or prayer.

8 The Path to Life

GATHERING AND PRAYER

(5 minutes)

VIDEO SEGMENT 8

(20 minutes)
Presenter: Deborah A. Appler

Prepare to View Video

Listen for ways the wisdom of Proverbs goes beyond the individual to the home and into the community.

View Video

Summary of video content:

Proverbs provides grounding in the midst of society's conflicting messages.

Proverbs presents practical wisdom on choices that take place in the context of relationships that begin in the home and extend into the larger community.

Proverbs cares about justice and righteousness.

The terms *paths, walking,* and *ways* demonstrate how one is instructed to move toward wisdom.

Discuss After Viewing Video

What wisdom does Proverbs offer the individual? What relationship do you see between wisdom practiced in the home and life in the community? Why do the terms *paths, walking,* and *ways* fit the subject of wisdom?

SCRIPTURE AND STUDY MANUAL

(50 minutes adults)   (35 minutes youth)

Read "Our Human Condition" silently. What assumptions about life and expectations of life underlie the ideas, thoughts, and attitudes expressed here? Talk in pairs. What response would the proverbs you read this week make to "Our Human Condition"?

Proverbs by their nature invite underlining or marking because they speak to our situation, call up a memory, or beckon us with their wisdom. In groups of three or four move quickly through daily notes and Scripture for Days 2–6, pausing to allow persons to identify particular Proverbs and say why they marked them. Allow opportunity for each person to speak. Then review the section "Form or Style," study manual page 64, and talk briefly about how that information aided understanding of Proverbs.

The study manual suggested choosing a theme and matching proverbs to the theme. Form pairs to hear another person's choice of theme and related proverbs. Then join another pair to share responses to locating proverbs that illustrate each of the Ten Commandments. Allow time for each person to identify connections between proverbs and the commandments. Respond to the question at the bottom of the right-hand column on study manual page 66.

Pray Psalm 25 together. If meeting space allows it, walk a path around the room as you read the psalm together.

BREAK

(10 minutes)

ENCOUNTER THE WORD

(40 minutes adults)   (20 minutes youth)

Scripture selection: Proverbs 22:17–23:18

This passage is part of a collection of proverbs designated "words of the wise." Read these words silently and work individually to identify and list the various themes addressed in the passage. Identify key words and repeated phrases. Then in groups of three or four hear what persons discovered in their study and discuss specific contexts where these proverbs apply today. Note also any proverbs that do not fit life in today's society.

MARKS OF FAITHFUL COMMUNITY

(20 minutes)

Being faithful community, we trust God's wisdom, not the world's wisdom, in making our choices.

Read the mark of faithful community aloud and look again at "Our Human Condition." What response is the mark of faithful community making to "Our Human Condition"? In groups of three respond to the three questions under "Marks of Faithful Community." Then hear each person respond to the question under "The Radical Disciple."

CLOSING AND PRAYER

(5 minutes adults)   (10 minutes youth)

Turn to Lesson 9 and check assignments. Write down prayer concerns. Close by praying the daily prayer from study manual page 62.

9 Destined to Die

GATHERING AND PRAYER

(5 minutes)

VIDEO SEGMENT 9

(20 minutes)
Presenter: Samuel Pagán

Prepare to View Video

Listen for the meanings of the word *vanity* and how Qoheleth attempts to make sense of life.

View Video

Summary of video content:

Ecclesiastes presents its message in concrete fashion, challenging the traditional Jewish wisdom and understanding of life.

Ecclesiastes is included in the Writings and aims at making sense through observation and experience.

Two truths stand out: God is ruler over all things, and everyone dies.

Discuss After Viewing Video

How does the word *vanity* convey Qoheleth's view of life? What is the central message of Ecclesiastes? Why do you think so little of the book is read in Christian churches?

SCRIPTURE AND STUDY MANUAL

(50 minutes adults)   (35 minutes youth)

Repeated throughout Ecclesiastes are the words *all, toil,* and *vanity.* Form three groups, assigning one word to each group. Instruct each group to (1) scan the Scriptures and their notes for Days 1–3 looking for their assigned word and (2) identify the specific ideas the writer wants to convey using that word. Then discuss these questions: What philosophy or view of life is the writer of Ecclesiastes attempting to counter or correct? How does the writer's repetition of this key word reinforce his message? What encouragement do you find in Ecclesiastes's discourse on life's futility?

Like the writer of Proverbs, the writer of Ecclesiastes has much to say about wisdom. Consider these passages: Ecclesiastes 1:12-18; 2:12-23; 7:5-14; 8:1-9; 9:13-18. In pairs or threes read one of the passages and talk about how the writer defines *wisdom.* Hear insights in the total group. Then compare the ways the writer of Ecclesiastes and the writer of Proverbs understand wisdom.

Ecclesiastes offers a stark picture of the realities of death. Hear these passages read aloud: 3:16–4:4; 9:1-6; 12:1-7. Once the passages have been read, invite persons to "talk back" to Qoheleth, responding to his understanding of death with their own understanding. Respond to the first question on study manual page 76. Close the discussion by reading Psalm 39:4-6 aloud in unison.

BREAK

(10 minutes)

ENCOUNTER THE WORD

(40 minutes adults)   (20 minutes youth)

Scripture selection: Ecclesiastes 5:1-7

Read aloud Ecclesiastes 5:1-7. Reread the passage silently with these questions in mind: What does this passage tell us about God? What does this passage tell us about human beings? What does this passage tell us about the relationship between God and human beings? Discuss in pairs or threes. Then in the total group discuss this question: If as the writer of Ecclesiastes observes, "All is vanity" (1:2), why is it important to "fear God" (5:7)? (See theological Bible study, pages 40–44 of *Teaching the Bible to Adults and Youth.*)

MARKS OF FAITHFUL COMMUNITY

(20 minutes)

Being faithful community, we accept life's mystery in all of its forms, and we accept death as a part of life.

Read aloud "Our Human Condition" and the mark of faithful community. Reflect individually on the first question under "Marks of Faithful Community" and then discuss it with a partner. Recall experiences that have helped you accept death as a part of life.

Read the first sentence in "The Radical Disciple." Again in pairs identify some of the things over which we have no control. Name some of the mysteries we encounter in life. Respond to the remaining questions under "Marks of Faithful Community."

CLOSING AND PRAYER

(5 minutes adults)   (10 minutes youth)

Turn to Lesson 10 and check assignments. Write down prayer concerns. Close by reading Ecclesiastes 3:1-8 aloud responsively.

10 Life Is a Gift

GATHERING AND PRAYER

(5 minutes)

VIDEO SEGMENT 10

(20 minutes)
Presenter: W. Sibley Towner

Prepare to View Video

Listen for the six assertions about God in Ecclesiastes and for what is missing in the writer's portrait of God.

View Video

Summary of video content:

We are not certain about the time, gender, or vocation behind the title *Qoheleth*.

We do know that the Teacher believed in God.

• God is the Sovereign Orderer of the world.
• We human beings cannot know what God does.
• Everything that happens is decreed by God.
• God made us free to choose good or ill and holds us responsible.
• God is to be feared—held in profoundest awe.
• God gives human beings the means to enjoy life and expects us to do it.

The book cautions against speaking too easily about who God is and what God will do.

Discuss After Viewing Video

Taking the six assertions about God as a whole, what one word best describes the God of Qoheleth? What do you think accounts for the missing elements in Ecclesiastes's portrait of God?

SCRIPTURE AND STUDY MANUAL

(50 minutes adults)   (35 minutes youth)

The writer of Ecclesiastes weaves his admonitions to enjoy life into his sober observations about life's futility. Examine four such passages: Ecclesiastes 2:22-26; 5:13-20; 8:14-17; 9:7-10. Form four groups to work through each of the four passages one by one, using these questions: What kind of enjoyment does the writer recommend? To what extent is one's enjoyment an answer to futility and absurdity? What part does God play in the enjoyment described?

Study manual page 84 suggests reading aloud some of the poetic passages in Ecclesiastes. Choose two or three to read in the total group. Then respond to the questions at the top of study manual page 85.

Consider Psalm 90 in the light of this week's reading of Ecclesiastes. In pairs or threes read the psalm silently. Then together identify words or phrases that echo those in Ecclesiastes. Compare the tone of Psalm 90 and the tone of Ecclesiastes: Which "voice" do you hear best? Say why. Conclude by singing "O God, Our Help in Ages Past."

BREAK

(10 minutes)

ENCOUNTER THE WORD

(40 minutes adults)   (20 minutes youth)

Scripture selection: Ecclesiastes 11

Read Ecclesiastes 11 aloud. Invite group members to reflect silently on the meaning of the passage. Use these questions to guide their reflection: What is the wisdom in not knowing the future? What are the advantages and disadvantages of not knowing "the work of God" (11:5)? How do we work and act with resourcefulness and generosity yet without anxiety over the results?

Invite persons individually to rewrite the passage in their own words, keeping in mind their reflection on the questions above. Hear everyone's paraphrase in the total group. (See paraphrasing, pages 71–76 of *Teaching the Bible to Adults and Youth*.)

MARKS OF FAITHFUL COMMUNITY

(20 minutes)

Being faithful community, we receive life as a gift, live it now, enjoy it, and thank God for it.

Read aloud "Our Human Condition." Read aloud the mark of faithful community. As a total group talk first about what causes people to resist moving from the situation described in "Our Human Condition" to the situation described in the mark of faithful community.

Then in pairs work through responses to the questions under "Marks of Faithful Community."

CLOSING AND PRAYER

(5 minutes adults)   (10 minutes youth)

Turn to Lesson 11 and check assignments. Write down prayer concerns. In keeping with "The Radical Disciple," close with a prayer of gratitude and trust.

11 A Just Complaint

GATHERING AND PRAYER

(5 minutes)

VIDEO SEGMENT 11

(20 minutes)
Presenter: Carol A. Newsom

Prepare to View Video

Listen for Israel's understanding of suffering and Job's thoughts about God.

View Video

Summary of video content:

The crucial question is, Why are people pious?

Israel did not think suffering was evidence of sin.

Israel made a distinction between sinful acts and being a truly wicked person.

God could be trusted to respond to anyone who called on God for help.

Job entertains the possibility that God has become his bitter enemy.

Job is grounded in the belief that God is just.

Discuss After Viewing Video

How did ancient Israel understand suffering? How has Job's experience of suffering affected his view of God?

SCRIPTURE AND STUDY MANUAL

(50 minutes adults)   (35 minutes youth)

Set the scene for studying Job by telling the story from Job 1–2. Divide the verses of the two chapters among the group members. Allow time for persons to review their assigned portions. Then tell the story.

Identify the main points the friends make in their counsel to Job and the main points Job makes in his replies. Work in pairs. Divide the Scriptures for Days 2 and 3 among the pairs as follows. Pair 1—Eliphaz (4–5); Pair 2—Job (6–7); Pair 3—Bildad (8); Pair 4—Job (9–10); Pair 5—Zophar (11); Pair 6—Job (12–14). Work in pairs for seven to ten minutes to prepare to present the main points in the assigned Scripture. Consult daily notes and the study manual. Then in the total group hear the friends present their counsel and Job's replies. Pair 1 will speak first for Eliphaz; Pair 2 will reply for Job. Each pair will speak in turn. In the total group respond to these questions: What sense do you have of the friends at this point? What sense of Job?

Continue the dialogue in the same fashion, assigning Scriptures for Days 4 and 5 to new pairs. Again allow seven to ten minutes for the pairs to prepare their comments. After hearing each pair speak, discuss these questions: How would you describe the attitude of the friends at this point in the dialogue? What is Job's state of mind at this point? Which of the explanations for suffering given by the friends have you heard given? Then respond to the question at the top of study manual page 93.

BREAK

(10 minutes)

ENCOUNTER THE WORD

(40 minutes adults)   (20 minutes youth)

Scripture selection: Job 3

Assign sections of Job 3 to three persons to read aloud: 3:1-10, 11-19, 20-26. In groups of three or four study the chapter for two purposes—to understand the feelings that underlie Job's words and to write a plea of mercy on Job's behalf. Use this question to guide Scripture study: What do you learn about Job's feelings from his choice of words and images? Talk about what sort of plea for mercy Job might make. Then individually, write a plea for mercy on Job's behalf. Hear the pleas in the groups.

MARKS OF FAITHFUL COMMUNITY

(20 minutes)

Being faithful community, we recognize the need to ask why when we experience suffering and injustice, and are assured of God's presence even when answers do not come.

Read "Our Human Condition" aloud. Then read the mark of faithful community. How does this statement address both our innocence about life and our recognition of the reality of life evident in "Our Human Condition"? Now in groups of three or four respond to the three questions in this section.

The radical disciple resists the urge to give pat answers. Why do you think pat answers come first to the tongue when tragedy strikes?

CLOSING AND PRAYER

(5 minutes adults)   (10 minutes youth)

Turn to Lesson 12 and check assignments. Write down prayer concerns. Close with Psalm 17:1-7.

12 On God's Terms

GATHERING AND PRAYER

(5 minutes)

VIDEO SEGMENT 12

(20 minutes)
Presenter: Carol A. Newsom

Prepare to View Video

Listen for how Job's unspoken assumptions about a trial and his understanding of the meaning of suffering limit his view of things. Pay attention to the way God reframes the issues.

View Video

Summary of video content:

Job's thinking about confrontation with God in terms of a legal trial is new.

God reframes the issues.

Job understands the world and his situation in terms of legal right and wrong.

God speaks of creation and of the chaotic.

God does not provide a rational explanation for suffering.

Discuss After Viewing Video

What are the problems with Job's model of a trial for solving his situation? What does God show Job about the world that he cannot see?

SCRIPTURE AND STUDY MANUAL

(50 minutes adults)   (35 minutes youth)

To have a sense of the whole debate, continue following the dialogue between Job's friends and Job begun last week. Divide Job 22–27 among six pairs who will prepare to speak for the friends or for Job. Hear from the pairs in chapter sequence. Then discuss this question: Where does the dialogue leave us in relation to the wicked, the righteous, and the justice of God?

Hear Job's beautiful yet sad words about his past and present situation by reading Job 29–30 aloud at a reasonably fast pace, with persons reading one verse in turn until the chapters are finished. For Job 29, stand (if possible) in a circle facing one another to read. For Job 30, stand in a circle facing away from one another to read. Then in groups of three or four, scan Job 31 and daily notes and talk about how Job asserts his integrity.

Refer the group to Elihu's speeches in Job 32–37.

Ask persons to suggest without comment ideas presented by Elihu not presented by the three friends.

Consider the mystery in creation. Divide Job 38:1–42:6 among four groups with the instruction to look for the mystery God points to in creation. Talk about what satisfies Job in God's speeches.

Conclude this part of your study of Job as you began it. Tell the conclusion of the story (42:7-17) around the circle.

BREAK

(10 minutes)

ENCOUNTER THE WORD

(40 minutes adults)   (20 minutes youth)
Scripture selection: Job 28

Turn Job 28 into a litany consisting of several statements, with each statement followed by a refrain on where wisdom is found. Form three groups to read Job 28 silently, to talk about the ideas they want to include in their litany and sentences that might serve as a refrain, and to write a litany. Allow plenty of time for discussing and writing the litanies. Then hear each group's litany.

MARKS OF FAITHFUL COMMUNITY

(20 minutes)

Being faithful community, we approach God with a sense of awe, accepting God's sovereignty, acknowledging life's mystery, and rejoicing in our place in God's creation.

Read "Our Human Condition" aloud and then consider the mark of faithful community's response phrase by phrase.

Look next at "The Radical Disciple." Sometimes learning comes by saying what something is not. Work in groups of three or four to turn the radical disciple statement into its opposite. For example, what is the opposite of trusting in God's purpose? What is the value in thinking in new ways? Discuss the first two questions under "Marks of Faithful Community" in the total group and the last questions in groups of three or four.

CLOSING AND PRAYER

(5 minutes adults)   (10 minutes youth)

Turn to Lesson 13 and check assignments. Write down prayer concerns. Pray Psalm 102:1-2.

13 Affairs of the Heart

GATHERING AND PRAYER

(5 minutes)

VIDEO SEGMENT 13

(20 minutes)
Presenter: Ellen F. Davis

Prepare to View Video

Listen for human desire both for sexual intimacy and intimacy with God, the healing of relationships damaged by disobedience in Eden.

View Video

Summary of video content:

The Song calls us to a deeper understanding of desire for sexual intimacy and for intimacy with God.

Song of Songs shows the healing of relationships between woman and man, between humanity and God, between humankind and nonhuman creatures.

Discuss After Viewing Video

What is your understanding of the idea that human desire for sexual intimacy and human desire for intimacy with God belong together? What three levels of meaning are addressed in the Song?

SCRIPTURE AND STUDY MANUAL

(50 minutes adults)   (35 minutes youth)

In two groups, recall language and images the man and woman in the Song of Solomon use to express their love to each other. Scan all the chapters. Then look at passages to compare language that expresses God's covenant love for Israel: Genesis 17:7-8; Exodus 6:7; Isaiah 54:4-8; 61:10-11; 62:5; Jeremiah 2:2; 31:31-32; Hosea 2:16-20. Discuss these questions: What are the messages carried in the language of love, whether between the man and the woman or between God and Israel? If language of human love can represent love between God and humanity, what does that say about human love?

Read Psalm 84 responsively. Talk about the ways love grows the more it is expressed, whether to God or to the lover.

Look at the Song from the perspective of wisdom literature. Form three groups and assign Scripture and questions as follows: Group 1—Day 3. What wisdom does Proverbs 2–3 offer the lovers in Song 5–6? Group 2—Day 4. What do you think the lovers in Song 7 hear in Proverbs 4–5? Group 3—

Day 5. What do Ecclesiastes 9 and 11 have to say to the lovers in Song 8?

BREAK

(10 minutes)

ENCOUNTER THE WORD

(40 minutes adults)   (20 minutes youth)

Scripture selection: Song of Solomon 1–8

Form four groups to study words, images, and scenes in the Song of Solomon. Assign each group two chapters. *Step 1:* Individually read the assigned chapters and list sights, sounds, tastes, smells, touches. Allow ten minutes for individual work. Talk in groups about what persons gained from Scripture through the senses. *Step 2:* Individually reread assigned chapters with these questions in mind: What do particular words, images, scenes remind me of from their use in other parts of the Old Testament? What words, images, scenes might point beyond these two lovers? Hear what persons discovered. Finally, discuss this question: What did you learn about how language can talk indirectly about God? (See using all the senses in Bible study, pages 57–61 of *Teaching the Bible to Adults and Youth.*)

MARKS OF FAITHFUL COMMUNITY

(20 minutes)

Being faithful community, we express and respond to the need and desire for intimacy by imitating God's lavish self-giving to us.

Read "Our Human Condition" aloud and invite examples or illustrations of the sentences in the statement. In pairs or threes discuss the third question under "Marks of Faithful Community." Read the mark of faithful community aloud and discuss this question: How is lavish self-giving a corrective to "Our Human Condition"?

Form new pairs to read "The Radical Disciple" and respond as each person feels comfortable. Finally, in the total group, discuss the first two questions in "Marks of Faithful Community."

CLOSING AND PRAYER

(5 minutes adults)   (10 minutes youth)

Turn to Lesson 14 and check assignments. Write down prayer concerns. Close with prayer.

14 Songs of Faith

GATHERING AND PRAYER

(5 minutes)

VIDEO SEGMENT 14

(25 minutes)
Presenter: Kenneth A. Kanter
Dancer: Diana Brown Holbert

Prepare to View Video

Listen for what is said about the Psalms as human documents reflecting human existence and about the psalmists' awareness of the presence of God.

View Video

Summary of video content:

Rabbinic literature designates the Psalms *Sefer Tellihim,* "The Book of Songs of Praise."

The Psalms are human documents that mirror existence.

Awareness of God was both intimate and all-pervading with the psalmists.

Discuss After Viewing Video

Where and why do we see ourselves in the Psalms? How would you describe the God addressed in the Psalms? What accounts for the universal appeal of the Psalms?

SCRIPTURE AND STUDY MANUAL

(50 minutes adults)   (35 minutes youth)

Begin by recalling learnings from "Fruit From the Tree of Life." In groups of three or four discuss these questions: What did you learn about how the Psalms were written and put together? How did this information increase your awareness of what you were reading?

Now, to get a sense of what characterizes particular kinds of psalms, form three groups to compare psalms within a psalm category. Group 1—*wisdom psalms:* 1; 112; Group 2—*psalms of lament:* 22; 88; 130; Group 3—*coronation psalms:* 2; 93; 95. Read the assigned psalms silently. Then use these questions to review and discuss the psalms: What similarities in language do you see? in feelings? in need? What sense do you get from these psalms of the relationship between the psalmist and God?

Learn from a communal prayer of lament to put your personal lament into words. Work individually. Read Psalm 74 silently, paying attention to this pattern: a cry for help and a plea to God to remember. Write a four-line lament that includes a cry and a plea to remember. Hear laments in the group.

In pairs examine the power in psalms. Assign each pair one of these psalms: 42; 57; 81; 90 with instructions to read the psalm silently, look for and try to sense its power, and discuss these questions: What gives the psalm its power? What allows this psalm to stand alone? Then ask each pair to join another pair to hear what each discovered.

Make the point we are selective in the psalms we read. Read "The Radical Disciple," study manual page 110, silently. Identify perceptions about Psalms that are barriers to owning all of the Psalms. What new understandings might overcome those barriers?

BREAK

(10 minutes)

ENCOUNTER THE WORD

(35 minutes adults)   (15 minutes youth)

Scripture selection: Psalm 103

Hear Psalm 103 read aloud. Work individually for 12 minutes. Read the psalm through three times to make notes on what it teaches us (1) about God, (2) about ourselves, (3) about the relationship between us and God. Then in groups of four, using notes from the three readings, discuss what the passage teaches us. (See theological Bible study, pages 40–44 of *Teaching the Bible to Adults and Youth.*)

MARKS OF FAITHFUL COMMUNITY

(20 minutes)

Being faithful community, we pray, knowing God welcomes us and knowing nothing we say or feel is outside that welcome.

Read "Our Human Condition" silently and reflect on times this statement is experienced as personally true, and why. In pairs talk about those reflections. Then hear each other's responses to the questions under "Marks of Faithful Community." Hear half the group read "Our Human Condition" and the other half respond with the mark of faithful community.

CLOSING AND PRAYER

(5 minutes adults)   (10 minutes youth)

Turn to Lesson 15 and check assignments. Write down prayer concerns. Sing "On Eagles' Wings."

15 Songs of Pain

GATHERING AND PRAYER

(5 minutes)

VIDEO SEGMENT 15

(30 minutes)
Presenter: Michael Jinkins
Dancer: Diana Brown Holbert

Prepare to View Video

Listen for the affirmation that the Lord reigns, for the unsettling nature of the psalms of lament.

View Video

Summary of video content:

The psalms of lament demand a reorientation of human life in relation to God.

In the world of the psalms, the reign of the Lord is absolute and comprehensive.

God is at the center rather than the self.

God does not immunize the faithful against difficulties; neither does God abandon the faithful.

Discuss After Viewing Video

What makes us uncomfortable with the biblical claim that the Lord reigns over every aspect of our lives? Why are the psalms of lament unsettling? How do the psalms of lament challenge our understanding of God and our relationship with God?

SCRIPTURE AND STUDY MANUAL

(45 minutes adults)   (30 minutes youth)

Examine the various elements of the psalms of lament. In groups of three or four review individual laments and notes for Day 1. Look for expressions of trust and mention of God's past actions in each psalm. Identify the lament pattern in the psalms. In the same groups, review community laments and notes for Day 2 and discuss these questions: Where do you see Israel's strong belief in a God of justice expressed in these psalms? What differences in tone and content do you see between the individual laments and the community laments?

"The Radical Disciple" called for writing a personal lament. Invite persons to form pairs or threes to hear personal laments and to talk about what they learned about themselves as they wrote their lament.

Hear Psalm 143 read aloud in the total group or read it in unison. Invite persons to tell briefly about their experience of making the psalm personal as

they prayed it daily. Now in pairs, turn to study manual page 123 and indicate to each other the psalm selected and why.

To examine the tendency to ignore difficult verses in the psalms, talk in two groups about "curses," study manual pages 122–23. How might our avoiding difficult psalms be influenced by desire to downplay the justice of God?

Examine psalms for Days 3–5 to see what they tell us about the nature of God. Form three groups to review psalms and daily notes and discuss related questions: Group 1—Day 3. What assurance do these psalms offer that God is a God who forgives? Group 2—Day 4. What assurance do these psalms offer that God is a God who can be trusted? Group 3—Day 5. What do these psalms tell us about God?

BREAK

(10 minutes)

ENCOUNTER THE WORD

(35 minutes adults)   (15 minutes youth)

Scripture selection: Psalm 139

Read Psalm 139 silently with these questions in mind: What does the psalm tell us about God? about women and men? about the relationship between God and human beings? Work individually on these questions and then discuss them one at a time in pairs or threes. (See theological Bible study, pages 40–41 of *Teaching the Bible to Adults and Youth*.)

MARKS OF FAITHFUL COMMUNITY

(20 minutes)

Being faithful community, we take God's Word with us into pain and trouble and let the psalms of lament be our voice.

Read "Our Human Condition." In pairs say when and why you have experienced this statement as true. What response does the mark of faithful community make to "Our Human Condition"?

In groups of three or four, hear responses to the questions in this section of the study manual.

CLOSING AND PRAYER

(5 minutes adults)   (10 minutes youth)

Turn to Lesson 16 and check assignments. Note "The Radical Disciple." Write down prayer concerns. Close with prayer.

16 Songs of Joy

GATHERING AND PRAYER

(5 minutes)

VIDEO SEGMENT 16

(20 minutes)
Presenters: John C. Holbert, Diana Brown Holbert

Prepare to View Video

Listen for reasons to praise God and for descriptions of justice and righteousness.

View Video

Summary of video content:

Every psalm of praise begins with the call to praise.

The God who does not die, who creates all there is, is faithful to God's creation.

The deeds of this God are particularly seen in mighty acts of justice.

"The righteous" are those who are committed to "justice."

Discuss After Viewing Video

Why is God worthy of praise? How would you describe the justice of God? Who are the righteous?

SCRIPTURE AND STUDY MANUAL

(50 minutes adults)   (35 minutes youth)

This week's suggestion for "The Radical Disciple" was to write a psalm of thanksgiving. Hear persons' psalms in the total group or in groups of three or four depending on how many wrote psalms.

Form three groups to consider how this week's psalms present the God we praise and the humans we are. Each group will scan Scripture and daily notes to discuss questions. Group 1—Day 1. What different words are used to describe God? What did you learn about people from these psalms? Group 2—Day 2. What is the basis for the psalmist's assurance the Lord will deliver? In what sense can we be sure God will rescue us when we cry to God? Group 3—Days 3 and 4. For Day 3: What are evidences of God's majesty and glory? What are examples of God's wisdom in creation? For Day 4: What images of trust, strength, and power do you see in these psalms? How would you describe the psalmist's own sense of his relationship to God?

Experience Psalms 113–118 (Egyptian Hallel) as Israel's remembering freedom from slavery. In the total group intersperse the reading aloud of Psalms 113–118 with recalling events in Israel's history. (Ask some persons ahead of time to be familiar with the following passages and to be ready to mention briefly [don't read] the events. Follow the sequence of the passages: Exodus 1:8-14; 12:21-27, 40-42; 14:19-31; 16:9-12; 17:1-6; 28:1-3; Deuteronomy 6:10-25; Joshua 3:14-17; 2 Chronicles 6:1-11.) After hearing the psalms and being reminded of the events, read in unison Psalm 122.

BREAK

(10 minutes)

ENCOUNTER THE WORD

(40 minutes adults)   (20 minutes youth)

Scripture selection: Psalm 107:1-32

Adapt the pattern of Psalm 107:1-32 to contemporary experiences of deliverance from troubles. Form four groups and assign one portion of the psalm to each group: 107:1-9, 10-16, 17-22, 23-32. Call attention to the pattern and wording in verses 6-8, which repeat in each of the other assigned portions. Instruct groups to study their assigned portion, to identify a contemporary experience of deliverance from trouble, and to write a psalm describing the experience and including the words and the pattern of the verses that repeat. Allow groups at least 20 minutes (10 minutes youth) for preparing their psalm. Hear each group's psalm without comment.

MARKS OF FAITHFUL COMMUNITY

(20 minutes)

Being faithful community, we praise God because God is worthy of praise, whatever our life situation.

In twos or threes, list favorite praise psalms as called for in this section and respond to the first two questions.

Next invite the group to read and reflect silently on "Our Human Condition" and the mark of faithful community. Then read the two statements aloud in unison. In groups of three or four respond to the last question in this section.

CLOSING AND PRAYER

(5 minutes adults)   (10 minutes youth)

Turn to Lesson 17 and review assignments. Write down prayer concerns. Close by reading Psalm 100.

Notes

DISCIPLE

JOHN
REVELATION

17 The Word Became a Human Being

Note to the teacher: Session 31 calls for use of a *DISCIPLE: UNDER THE TREE OF LIFE Revelation Video Letter* that you must order from the DISCIPLE office. See teacher helps pages 11–13 for information on the video, a description of the letter, and procedure for ordering the letter. Order now.

GATHERING AND PRAYER

(5 minutes)

VIDEO SEGMENT 17

(20 minutes)
Presenter: Ben Witherington, III

Prepare to View Video

Listen for what it means to call Jesus the Word of God and how John draws on Greek and Hebrew ideas of wisdom.

View Video
Summary of video content:

John 1:1-18 was written to answer the question, Who is Jesus?

Many persons seek Jesus, trying to find out who he is; the difficulty is that none knows what the reader knows—Jesus is the incarnation of the Word of God.

John's use of *Logos* to refer to Jesus recalls the Creation story.

Discuss After Viewing Video

What do you think John wants to say by calling Jesus the Word of God? How does John use Greek and Hebrew ideas about wisdom to reveal Jesus' identity?

SCRIPTURE AND STUDY MANUAL

(50 minutes adults)   (35 minutes youth)

Recalling the Scripture and daily notes, study John 1 in three sections. Allow about fifteen minutes per section.

(1) *The Prologue:* 1:1-18. Scan the account of Creation in Genesis 1 and the giving of the Law in Exodus 20. How does the Prologue's use of the term *logos* (word) draw upon the concept of God's word as depicted in Genesis and Exodus?

(2) *The testimony of John:* 1:19-34. Why does the Prologue establish John the Baptist's identity before introducing Jesus?

(3) *The testimony of the first disciples:* 1:35-51. Jesus' first words in John are "What are you looking for?" What did Jesus want the two disciples of John the Baptist to hear in that question? What did John want his readers to hear in that question?

When Jesus says "Come and see" (1:39), what is Jesus inviting his disciples to do? What is John inviting his readers to understand about the nature of discipleship? In pairs hear the paragraph written in response to the instruction at the top of study manual page 139.

BREAK

(10 minutes)

ENCOUNTER THE WORD

(40 minutes adults)   (20 minutes youth)
Scripture selection: John 1:43-51

Read John 1:43-51 as a dialogue, assigning persons to be the narrator, Jesus, Philip, and Nathanael. Read the passage again silently. Then as a total group, identify the names for Jesus mentioned in the passage. Form two groups to discuss these questions: What do the various names reveal about who the first disciples think Jesus is? What does the name Jesus gives to himself in 1:51 reveal about who he is?

MARKS OF FAITHFUL COMMUNITY

(20 minutes)

Being faithful community, we receive and claim the teaching of the community that Jesus is God in the flesh.

Read aloud "Our Human Condition" and the mark of faithful community. Read John 1:14 aloud from study manual page 134. In what ways has or does the teaching that Jesus is God in the flesh put you on the defensive? Hear responses to the questions under "Marks of Faithful Community."

"The Radical Disciple": What issues related to living in a pluralistic society challenge our belief that Jesus is the unique Word of God?

CLOSING AND PRAYER

(5 minutes adults)   (10 minutes youth)

Turn to Lesson 18 and check assignments. Write down prayer concerns. Close by praying aloud Psalm 33:1-9.

18 Born of Water and Spirit

GATHERING AND PRAYER

(5 minutes)

VIDEO SEGMENT 18

(20 minutes)
Presenter: Marianne Meye Thompson

Prepare to View Video

Note what the word *sign* means in John and why he uses that word to describe the miracles and works of Jesus.

View Video

Summary of video content:

The miracles or works of Jesus function as signs because they point beyond themselves.

Two levels of perception in seeing a sign are "sight" and "insight."

Jesus' deeds are manifestations of God's life-giving power in and through him.

Discuss After Viewing Video

How do the works of Jesus function as signs in John? What kind of belief do the signs call for? What "sight and insight" comes from the sign of Jesus turning water into wine?

SCRIPTURE AND STUDY MANUAL

(50 minutes adults)   (35 minutes youth)

This week's Scriptures are framed by Jesus' first two signs. Form two or three groups to compare John 2:1-11 and 4:46-54, using these questions: What elements do the passages have in common? How do they differ? How do the details help to convey the meaning of the signs? In each of the passages, what does Jesus offer those who witness his miraculous sign? What evidence does John give of belief in Jesus resulting from what Jesus accomplishes with these first two signs?

In John, Jesus' first extended conversations are with two individuals—Nicodemus (3:1-21) and the Samaritan woman (4:7-42). Work in pairs with each of the conversations, one at a time, following these steps: (1) Scan the passage and daily notes. (2) Describe the occasion or setting of the conversation. (3) Explore the content of the conversation between Jesus and each individual. What change takes place in each character's understanding of Jesus over the course of the conversation? What images does Jesus use and how are they appropriate to each person? (4) Discuss John's purpose. What aspect of Jesus' identity is clarified through each conversation?

In the total group discuss this question: How would you describe the faith of Nicodemus and the Samaritan woman based on their conversations with Jesus?

If anyone did research on the various interpretations of John 3:5, hear reports.

BREAK

(10 minutes)

ENCOUNTER THE WORD

(40 minutes adults)   (20 minutes youth)

Scripture selection: John 2:13-22

Read John 2:13-22 aloud. Then hear the parallel accounts of Jesus' cleansing the Temple in Matthew 21:12-13; Mark 11:15-17; and Luke 19:45-46. Compare the four passages, making notes on similarities and differences in the Synoptic accounts and John's account. Pay attention to the chronology of the event, the details given, and the words Jesus speaks. Then in threes or fours talk about what you discovered. Discuss this question: What message about Jesus do you think John intended to convey in the way he tells the story of Jesus' cleansing the Temple?

MARKS OF FAITHFUL COMMUNITY

(20 minutes)

Being faithful community, we see life as both physical and spiritual, and while we exist in the physical, we live in new life graciously offered by God in Jesus Christ.

Read aloud "Our Human Condition" and the mark of faithful community. How does the new life offered by God in Jesus give purpose both to our living and to our dying? With a partner talk about responses to the questions under "Marks of Faithful Community."

Read the first statement in "The Radical Disciple" paragraph and discuss the question that follows.

CLOSING AND PRAYER

(5 minutes adults)   (10 minutes youth)

Turn to Lesson 19 and check assignments. Write down prayer concerns. Close by singing together the hymn "Lift Up Your Heads, Ye Mighty Gates."

19 Bread of Life

GATHERING AND PRAYER

(5 minutes)

VIDEO SEGMENT 19

(25 minutes)
Presenter: Richard B. Hays

Prepare to View Video

Pay attention to what the "I am" speeches of Jesus reveal in John's Gospel. Note the connections between the manna story and Jesus' miraculous feeding of the crowd in John 6.

View Video

Summary of video content:

In John's Gospel Jesus delivers long discourses about himself and his mission.

Several of those speeches begin with the words *ego eimi:* "I am."

John 6 is where the first "I am" speeches appear.

The people see the miraculous feeding as a sign like the provision of manna in the wilderness.

Jesus is the bread that has come down from heaven.

Discuss After Viewing Video

How does the manna story illuminate Jesus' miraculous feeding of the crowd? What about Jesus' declaration, "I am the bread of life," offended those who opposed him?

SCRIPTURE AND STUDY MANUAL

(50 minutes adults)   (35 minutes youth)

Pay attention in these chapters to both the works Jesus does and the words Jesus speaks to explain those works. Begin by examining Jesus' healing of the lame man. In groups of three or four, first discuss the healing (5:1-18): How does this healing compare to Jesus' healing of the official's son in 4:46-53? How does the lame man respond to being healed? What is the meaning of the statement Jesus makes to the lame man in 5:14? Next discuss the discourse (5:19-24): In what ways is Jesus' healing of the lame man an affront to the Jewish authorities? How does Jesus' appeal to his authority as Son of God answer the criticism described in 5:18?

Explore John 6 by focusing first on the miraculous feeding in 6:1-15. Compare the passage with parallels in the Synoptics (Matthew 14:13-21; Mark 6:34-44; Luke 9:12-17). In pairs identify what is unique about John's account. Notice the details: What does Jesus do and how? What does Jesus say? What do the disciples do? How does the crowd respond to the miracle? Discuss this question: What does the sign of the miraculous feeding reveal about Jesus?

Now work through Jesus' discourses in John 6 by dividing them among five groups: Group 1—6:22-34; Group 2—6:35-40; Group 3—6:41-51; Group 4—6:52-59; Group 5—6:60-71. Read the assigned passage and discuss it using these questions: To what group of hearers does Jesus speak? How does John characterize this group? How does Jesus' claim to be "the bread of life" address the misunderstanding or protest of his hearers?

BREAK

(10 minutes)

ENCOUNTER THE WORD

(35 minutes adults)   (15 minutes youth)

Scripture selection: John 5:30-47

Hear John 5:30-47 read aloud. Then individually reread the passage with these questions in mind: Who does Jesus say he is? Who does Jesus say God is in relationship to him? Who does Jesus say human beings are in relationship to him? Discuss responses in pairs. As a total group talk about this question: What message does this passage convey to believers in our day?

MARKS OF FAITHFUL COMMUNITY

(20 minutes)

Being faithful community, we seek nothing less than "the food that endures for eternal life," Jesus the living bread.

Read aloud "Our Human Condition" and the mark of faithful community. What causes us to seek something *less than* Jesus the living bread to satisfy our deepest hungers? Respond to the last two questions under this section and then to the first three.

Conclude by hearing responses to the question under "The Radical Disciple."

CLOSING AND PRAYER

(5 minutes adults)   (10 minutes youth)

Turn to Lesson 20 and check assignments. Write down prayer concerns. Close by sharing fresh bread together and praying Psalm 65.

20 Light of the World

GATHERING AND PRAYER

(5 minutes)

VIDEO SEGMENT 20

(20 minutes)
Presenter: D. Moody Smith, Jr.

Prepare to View Video

Listen for whom John refers to by the phrase "the Jews" and for what characterizes their opposition to Jesus.

View Video

Summary of video content:

In the Gospel of John, Jesus is repeatedly involved in controversy with opponents, usually called "the Jews."

These opponents challenge his claims about his role, authority, and mission, but particularly his relationship to God.

"The Jews" in John are different from the Jewish people.

Discuss After Viewing Video

Who are "the Jews" in John's Gospel? What distinguished "the Jews" from other Jews in John? What about Jesus did "the Jews" reject?

SCRIPTURE AND STUDY MANUAL

(50 minutes adults)   (35 minutes youth)

Jesus' claims about himself and his works continue to cause controversy, reaching a climax in John 7—8. Form four groups to examine portions of Jesus' dialogue in the Temple: Group 1—7:1-36; Group 2—7:37-52; Group 3—8:12-30; Group 4—8:31-59. Scan the passages to answer these questions: Whom does Jesus address? What claims does Jesus make about himself? Why do his hearers question or object to Jesus' claims?

Have two groups join to discuss how Jesus uses Abraham to criticize his opponents and authenticate his purpose in 8:31-59. What does Jesus mean by saying, "Before Abraham was, I am"?

As a total group recall the descriptions of the Feast of Booths in the study manual. Then discuss these questions: Taken together, what do Jesus' claims to be water (7:37-39) and light (8:12) say about his relationship with God? with the world? with the believer?

Read the story of Jesus and the blind man as a drama, assigning parts to group members (Jesus, the disciples, the blind man, the Pharisees, the parents of the blind man, narrator). Pay attention to plot development, dialogue, instances of irony. Discuss how the ironies help convey the message of the passage. Compare the gradual journey of the blind man from blindness to sight with the descent of the Pharisees from sight to blindness. What works and words of Jesus blind the eyes of the Pharisees? How do their views of sin and sabbath contribute to their blindness?

BREAK

(10 minutes)

ENCOUNTER THE WORD

(40 minutes adults)   (20 minutes youth)

Scripture selection: John 7:53–8:11

Hear John 7:53–8:11 read aloud. Then read the passage again using these questions as a guide: What does this story say about who Jesus is? What does this story say about the "scribes and Pharisees"? about the adulterous woman? How does this story illuminate the conflict between Jesus and "the Jews"?

MARKS OF FAITHFUL COMMUNITY

(20 minutes)

Being faithful community, we choose to be diligent witnesses to the light of Christ.

Read aloud "Our Human Condition" and the mark of faithful community. Consider this question with a partner: What are some things we must let go of in our lives in order to choose to be witnesses to the light of Christ? Hear responses to the questions under "Marks of Faithful Community."

"The Radical Disciple": Talk about some of your decisions about where, how, and to whom to take the light of Christ. Agree on how to hold one another accountable for those decisions.

CLOSING AND PRAYER

(5 minutes adults)   (10 minutes youth)

Turn to Lesson 21 and check assignments. Write down prayer concerns. Light a candle and pray Psalm 27 in closing.

21 The Coming Hour

Reminder: If you have not ordered the *DISCIPLE: UNDER THE TREE OF LIFE Revelation Video Letter* for Session 31, order now. See teacher helps page 12 for description of the letter and ordering procedure.

GATHERING AND PRAYER

(5 minutes)

VIDEO SEGMENT 21

(20 minutes)
Presenter: Sharon H. Ringe

Prepare to View Video

Listen for who or what contributes to our understanding of Jesus as the resurrection in the story of the raising of Lazarus.

View Video

Summary of video content:

The "sign" of raising Lazarus is the final one before Jesus himself becomes the ultimate "sign" of God's power; both signs deal with life and death.

The understanding in Jesus' day was that the dead remained in Sheol to wait until the time of resurrection; Lazarus is not resurrected in that sense.

Jesus identifies himself as "the resurrection and the life," embodying both the power of that decisive moment of awakening and also the verdict in favor of the life that conquers death forever.

Discuss After Viewing Video

How do Martha's confession that Jesus is the Messiah (11:27) and the raising of Lazarus (11:44) help us understand Jesus' claim to be "the resurrection and the life"?

SCRIPTURE AND STUDY MANUAL

(50 minutes adults)   (35 minutes youth)

The feasts of Dedication and Passover provide the backdrop for this week's readings. Recall rituals and symbols associated with the two festivals and what each commemorated (study manual pages 164 and 166). Then scan John 10:22–12:50 to list (1) what Jesus says about himself and (2) what he does. Discuss this question: What meaning do the festivals give to Jesus' words and actions in these passages?

Form groups of three or four to explore Jesus' raising of Lazarus in John 11:1-44. *First,* examine the story's structure. Who are the main characters and what roles do they play in the narrative? What happens in the story and in what sequence? What is the climax? *Second,* identify examples of Jesus' being misunderstood by his disciples, by Martha, by Mary, and by the other Jews. Why do you think John wants to show people misunderstanding Jesus' words and works? *Third,* discuss the meaning of the sign. What does Jesus' raising of Lazarus say about death? about who Jesus is? about God's purpose in the world? about the life of the believer?

BREAK

(10 minutes)

ENCOUNTER THE WORD

(40 minutes adults)   (20 minutes youth)
Scripture selection: John 12:1-11

Invite group members to close their eyes as someone reads John 12:1-11 aloud and imagine themselves at the home of Mary and Martha, eating dinner with Jesus and Lazarus. Listen for sights, sounds, smells, tastes, and touches. Then read the passage silently and work individually to list insights that came to you through your senses. Talk through the passage and the list with a partner. What new insights did you gain from hearing the story from the perspective of all the senses? (See using all the senses in Bible study, pages 57–61 of *Teaching the Bible to Adults and Youth*.)

MARKS OF FAITHFUL COMMUNITY

(20 minutes)

Being faithful community, we live and die believing Jesus is the Messiah, the Son of God.

Read aloud "Our Human Condition." Then read silently the first paragraph under "Marks of Faithful Community." Read aloud the mark of faithful community. Hear responses to the questions in the "Marks of Faithful Community" section.

Read aloud John 12:24 in "The Radical Disciple." As a total group, hear responses to the related question.

CLOSING AND PRAYER

(5 minutes adults)   (10 minutes youth)

Turn to Lesson 22 and check assignments. Write down prayer concerns. Close by praying Psalm 116:1-4.

22 Power to Bear Fruit

GATHERING AND PRAYER

(5 minutes)

VIDEO SEGMENT 22

(20 minutes)
Presenter: Koo Yong Na

Prepare to View Video
    Listen for ways to understand the meaning of Jesus' act of footwashing.

View Video
Summary of video content:
    All four Gospels record Jesus' sharing the Last Supper, but John is unique in putting emphasis on Jesus' washing his disciples' feet.
• In John 13:1-11 Jesus' act of footwashing became essential to the gaining of heritage with him.
• In John 13:12-20 Jesus washed the feet of his disciples as an example of self-sacrificing humility.
    Jesus makes clear that what he is doing in the act of footwashing is inviting the disciples to share in his life and death.

Discuss After Viewing Video
    Identify various ways to understand Jesus' act of footwashing. What is the connection between the footwashing and Jesus' death?

SCRIPTURE AND STUDY MANUAL

(50 minutes adults)   (35 minutes youth)
    Look further into the meaning of the footwashing by examining the two conversations between Jesus and Peter in John 13. Form two groups. Group 1—Read 13:6-10 and discuss these questions: What do the three statements by Peter (13:6, 8, 9) reveal about his understanding of the footwashing? What do the three responses from Jesus (13:7, 8, 10) reveal about what he wanted Peter to understand about the footwashing? Group 2—Read 13:31-38 and discuss these questions: In light of Peter's questions, what does he want from Jesus? In light of Jesus' responses, what does he want from Peter and the other disciples?
    Together talk about why John highlights Peter's lack of understanding of Jesus' words and actions during the Last Supper.
    Review the section entitled "The Paraclete" on study manual page 176. According to Jesus' description of the Paraclete's functions (14:15-17,

26; 15:26; 16:5-14), what will a community who receives the gift of Jesus' Spirit look like?
    Explore the themes of Jesus' farewell speech and prayer in John 14–17. In groups of three or four, scan the four chapters to identify what Jesus says about the believers' relation to Christ, to one another, and to the world. Discuss this question: Which of Jesus' words would you say are most challenging to his disciples? Which are most comforting?

BREAK

(10 minutes)

ENCOUNTER THE WORD

(40 minutes adults)   (20 minutes youth)
    Scripture selection: John 14:1-14
    Read John 14:1-14 aloud. In pairs discuss these questions: What message do you hear in this passage? What feelings does this passage evoke? What have you heard the church teach about this passage? How does the Scripture and the church's teaching on it inform your understanding of what relationship to God means? How do you resolve differences in your thinking and the church's teaching on this passage? (See shared praxis, pages 45–50 of *Teaching the Bible to Adults and Youth*.)

MARKS OF FAITHFUL COMMUNITY

(20 minutes)
    Being faithful community, we abide in Christ in order to bear the fruit of service.
    Read aloud "Our Human Condition" and then reflect silently on the word(s) or phrase(s) that are true in your experience. Read aloud the mark of faithful community. With a partner talk about how a relationship of fruitful service to Christ is an answer to the situation described in "Our Human Condition." Describe for each other the act of servanthood you identified in response to "The Radical Disciple" on study manual page 170.
    Hear responses to the three questions under "Marks of Faithful Community."

CLOSING AND PRAYER

(5 minutes adults)   (10 minutes youth)
    Turn to Lesson 23 and check assignments. Write down prayer concerns. Close by praying Psalm 80:14-19.

23 Where No One Else Can Go

GATHERING AND PRAYER

(5 minutes)

VIDEO SEGMENT 23

(25 minutes)
Presenter: R. Alan Culpepper

Prepare to View Video
Note the key elements of John's account of Jesus' death and listen for how they underscore the meaning of the cross for the church.

View Video
Summary of video content:
John 18 and 19 are the heart of the Gospel.
John gives the most detailed account of Jesus' trial before Pilate, arranged in seven scenes.
John's account of the death of Jesus is different from the Synoptic accounts.
Through his account of Jesus' death, John shows that a new community was constituted at the cross.
What happened at the cross shapes for all time the nature and design of the church.

Discuss After Viewing Video
What understanding of the church does John develop in his account of Jesus' death? To what extent does Jesus' death on the cross shape the nature and design of your church?

SCRIPTURE AND STUDY MANUAL

(50 minutes adults)   (35 minutes youth)
Jesus' "hour" finally comes in John 18–19. Begin a study of Jesus' death by hearing these verses read aloud: John 2:4; 7:30; 8:20; 13:1. Then recall assigned readings and daily notes for Days 1–3 to respond to these questions: What evidence do you find in John 18–19 that Jesus is in control of the events of his "hour"? How does this evidence shape your understanding of the purpose of Jesus' death?
Read aloud the drama of Jesus' crucifixion in John 19:1-37. Assign persons the parts of the narrator, Jesus, and Pilate. Have everyone read in unison all the other parts. After the reading, talk about how Jesus, Pilate, and the Jewish leaders come across in the story. Now hear each person in turn say what the cross means or signifies in John. Then hear from those who followed the instruction in "The Radical Disciple."

John identifies four women and the beloved disciple "standing near the cross." Imagine you are one of those close to Jesus in life, who has just witnessed his death. Write a lament expressing to God the feelings you have at this moment. Recall that Mark tells us Psalm 22:1 was on the lips of the dying Jesus. Remember your daily reading of Psalm 22. Use its language as your guide.

BREAK

(10 minutes)

ENCOUNTER THE WORD

(35 minutes adults)   (15 minutes youth)
Scripture selection: John 18:28-38
Read aloud the conversation between Jesus and Pilate. Read the passage again silently and work individually on these questions: What do you think John intended this passage to say to the first hearers? What does this passage say to the church today? to our world? to you? Talk about your responses with a partner. Then discuss this question: How does John's Gospel answer Pilate's question, What is truth? (See depth Bible study, pages 35–39 of *Teaching the Bible to Adults and Youth.*)

MARKS OF FAITHFUL COMMUNITY

(20 minutes)
Being faithful community, we receive with gratitude the selfless love of God in Christ shown on the cross and proclaim it in our living.
Read aloud "Our Human Condition." Respond to this question in pairs: When is it difficult for you to receive selfless love from another human being? Read aloud the mark of faithful community. Discuss this question: When is it difficult for you to receive the selfless love of God as shown on the cross?
Read the second paragraph under "Marks of Faithful Community" and talk about your responses to the question there.

CLOSING AND PRAYER

(5 minutes adults)   (10 minutes youth)
Turn to Lesson 24 and check assignments. Write down prayer concerns. Close by inviting group members, one by one, to pray aloud the laments they wrote earlier in the session.

24 Weeping Turned to Witness

GATHERING AND PRAYER

(5 minutes)

VIDEO SEGMENT 24

(20 minutes)
Presenter: R. Grace Jones Imathiu

Prepare to View Video

Notice how the first witnesses to the empty tomb struggle to understand and believe what they see.

View Video

Summary of video content:

Mary misunderstands what she sees in the empty tomb; she is mourning the loss of Jesus' body.

Only after Jesus speaks Mary's name does Mary understand she has been seeking the wrong Jesus.

Jesus' command to the first witness to his resurrection is to not hold on to who he was but to go and tell others who he is.

For John, disciples of Jesus must confront the message of the empty tomb.

Discuss After Viewing Video

What causes Mary to move from misunderstanding the reality of the empty tomb to proclaiming "I have seen the Lord"? What about the message of the empty tomb confirms your belief in the risen Lord?

SCRIPTURE AND STUDY MANUAL

(50 minutes adults)   (35 minutes youth)

Scan assigned readings and daily notes for Day 1 to compare all four Gospel accounts of the empty tomb. In groups of three or four discuss those elements that distinguish John's account from the Synoptic accounts. Why do you think John included certain details not found in the other accounts? What does Jesus mean by instructing Mary to tell the other disciples that he is ascending to the Father rather than that he has risen?

Next compare a post-Resurrection appearance of Jesus in John with one from each Synoptic Gospel. Form three groups. Have groups read John 20:26-29 and one of these passages: Matthew 28:16-20; Mark 16:12-20; Luke 24:36-43. Use these questions to compare the assigned passage with the John passage: What happens? Who is present to see Jesus? What does Jesus say and do? What evidence is there of anyone responding to Jesus' presence with belief?

Now work with John 21. Recall the Scripture and review daily notes for Day 4. Consider Jesus' works—the miraculous catch and the giving of bread and fish. What message does this story convey to those who would make up the community of believers? Consider Jesus' words to Peter—"Feed my sheep. . . . Follow me." What do Jesus' commands to Peter say to those who would be his disciples? In pairs hear responses to the question at the top of study manual page 191.

BREAK

(10 minutes)

ENCOUNTER THE WORD

(40 minutes adults)   (20 minutes youth)

Scripture selection: John 20:19-25

Read John 20:19-25 aloud as others follow in their Bibles. Work individually on these questions: What does this passage say? What does John intend this passage to communicate to its first hearers? What situation might this passage have been addressing? What does this Scripture say to believers today? What does it say to you? What do you say to the Scripture? What claims does the risen Christ make on us in this passage? (See dialogue and encounter, pages 51–56 of *Teaching the Bible to Adults and Youth*.)

MARKS OF FAITHFUL COMMUNITY

(20 minutes)

Being faithful community, we believe in the resurrected Christ and witness boldly to that victory with joy.

Read aloud "Our Human Condition" and the mark of faithful community. How do you experience the tension between those two statements? Discuss the questions under "Marks of Faithful Community."

"The Radical Disciple": Where will you risk taking the good news of the empty tomb?

CLOSING AND PRAYER

(5 minutes adults)   (10 minutes youth)

Turn to Lesson 25 and check assignments. Write down prayer concerns. Close by praying aloud Psalm 98. Invite persons who developed hand motions to go with the psalm to accompany the group's praying.

25 Our Life Together

GATHERING AND PRAYER

(5 minutes)

VIDEO SEGMENT 25

(25 minutes)
Presenter: Charles H. Talbert

Prepare to View Video

Listen for proposed solutions to a disagreement over christology (belief) and ethics (behavior), particularly the appeal to the Christian past.

View Video

Summary of video content:

The letters of John trace a disagreement in the early church over christology and ethics.

The elder has two solutions: Hold the Christian past as authoritative and deny access to teachers who hold other positions.

The opponents denied the humanity of the church's Savior, a heresy called *docetism,* and believed themselves free from moral law.

Discuss After Viewing Video

What solutions to the problems of christology and ethics does the author propose?

SCRIPTURE AND STUDY MANUAL

(50 minutes adults)   (35 minutes youth)

In groups of three or four study Romans 14 and Ephesians 4:1-16 to see what they say about unity in the body of Christ. What contributes to or threatens unity in the body? What is the place of the individual in the body? What is the responsibility of the individual to other members of the body?

Read Psalm 133 in unison. Invite persons to identify expressions of unity in your congregation that are experienced as blessing. Hear responses to the question on study manual page 195.

Use questions and words to guide study of passages from First John. Form two groups and make these assignments: Group 1—Day 2; Group 2—Day 3. Both groups will use these questions: What is being said about Jesus Christ? How do these chapters portray those who belong to God and those who do not? Next say what you think John means specifically in his recurring use of these words: *sin, truth, abide, light, darkness, the world, antichrist, lawlessness, commandment, testimony.*

What counsel do the writers of Second and Third John and Jude (Days 4 and 5) give for responding to lack of unity in the church and to persons who cause division in the church? Discuss in groups of three or four. Hear responses to the questions on study manual pages 197 and 198.

BREAK

(10 minutes)

ENCOUNTER THE WORD

(35 minutes adults)   (15 minutes youth)

Scripture selection: 1 John 1

Hear 1 John 1 read aloud. In groups of three or four talk through 1 John 1 verse by verse using these questions: What do the words say? What do they mean? What is behind the words? How do you understand the images and where have these images appeared before? What do you think the author intends to say? Then ask persons to individually put 1 John 1 into their own words. Allow about twenty minutes for this paraphrasing. Hear the paraphrases in the groups. (See paraphrasing, pages 71–76 of *Teaching the Bible to Adults and Youth.*)

MARKS OF FAITHFUL COMMUNITY

(20 minutes)

Being faithful community, we are shaped in our relationship to one another by the message we have heard from the beginning: Love one another.

Read "Our Human Condition" aloud. What is the issue or concern underlying the questions in "Our Human Condition"? Read the mark of faithful community. What is the overriding significance of the command to love one another?

In groups of three or four discuss the first three questions in this section. Then discuss the last two questions in the total group.

To what would the radical disciple appeal in holding self and community to the central teaching about Christ? What questions and opposition would the radical disciple face in the church?

CLOSING AND PRAYER

(5 minutes adults)   (10 minutes youth)

Turn to Lesson 26 and check assignments. Note "The Radical Disciple." Write down prayer concerns. Read Jude 24-25 as a closing benediction.

26 The Power of the Tongue

Have you ordered the *DISCIPLE: UNDER THE TREE OF LIFE Revelation Video Letter* for Session 31? See teacher helps page 12 for ordering procedure.

GATHERING AND PRAYER

(5 minutes)

VIDEO SEGMENT 26

(20 minutes)
Presenter: Zan W. Holmes, Jr.

Prepare to View Video

Give attention to James as wisdom literature and to the relationship of faith and works.

View Video

Summary of video content:

James expresses concern about how Christians are to behave in relation to one another.

James presents a contrast between two types of wisdom—human wisdom and wisdom from above.

One particular mark of wisdom in James is consistency between words and deeds.

Discuss After Viewing Video

In what ways is James similar to traditional wisdom literature? What relationship do you see between faith and works and a life of wholeness and integrity?

SCRIPTURE AND STUDY MANUAL

(50 minutes adults)   (35 minutes youth)

Wisdom often takes the form of proverbs, and since James is a Christian wisdom book, create some proverbs to express the teachings in James 1–4. Form four groups and assign one chapter to each group with these instructions: Talk through the chapter a verse or section at a time to understand what James is saying. Refer also to daily notes. Then choose at least three teachings from the chapter that are crucial to understanding James to put into proverb form. Refresh your understanding of how content is put together in a proverb by looking at examples in Proverbs 10–15. Then work together to write three proverbs expressing the three teachings. Groups will need at least twenty minutes to study their assigned chapter and prepare their proverbs. In the total group hear each group's proverbs, starting with James 1.

In groups of three or four discuss the various ways James 5 is calling the community to accountability. Then hear one another's responses to the questions on study manual page 206.

Call attention to "The Radical Disciple," study manual page 200. Talk about what persons heard, what they became aware of in their personal use of language and ways of talking, and of the relationship they see between their faith and their speech.

As a total group consider the suggestion under "If You Want to Know More."

BREAK

(10 minutes)

ENCOUNTER THE WORD

(40 minutes adults)   (20 minutes youth)

Scripture selection: James 1:12-27

Invite the group to read James 1:12-27 as if for the first time looking for new insights or becoming aware of questions not thought of earlier. In pairs discuss these questions: What does the text say? What do you think James wished to say for God? What meaning does this passage have for us today? Then work individually on this question: If I take this passage seriously, what changes would I have to make in my life? Respond in turn to the question. (See depth Bible study, pages 35–39 of *Teaching the Bible to Adults and Youth*.)

MARKS OF FAITHFUL COMMUNITY

(20 minutes)

Being faithful community, we recognize words have power to build up or destroy. Therefore, we do not take lightly the use of our tongue.

In the total group read "Our Human Condition" aloud and discuss this question: What attitudes are evident in this statement that we may think of as harmless? What counsel does the mark of faithful community give to the description of us and our actions in "Our Human Condition"?

In pairs or threes respond to the questions in this section of the study manual.

CLOSING AND PRAYER

(5 minutes adults)   (10 minutes youth)

Turn to Lesson 27 and check assignments. Write down prayer concerns. In closing read James 3:5-6 and pray the daily prayer on study manual page 200.

27 Vision of End Time

Reminder: See teacher helps page 12 for ordering the *DISCIPLE: UNDER THE TREE OF LIFE Revelation Video Letter* for Session 31.

GATHERING AND PRAYER

(5 minutes)

VIDEO SEGMENT 27

(30 minutes)
Presenter: M. Eugene Boring
Scripture: Marquis Laughlin

Prepare to View Video

Two competing claims faced the Christians addressed by Revelation: The claim of the one God and the claim of emperor worship. Listen for the tension in those claims.

View Video

Summary of video content:
Revelation emphasizes faith in the one God who makes exclusive claims.

Domitian, the Roman emperor, insisted on being addressed as "our Lord and God the emperor."

Many Christians saw the demand for emperor worship as a harmless ritual to which they could adjust without compromising their faith.

Discuss After Viewing Video

Describe the situation created for Christians by the claims of their God and the claims of their government and culture. What claims of our culture tempt us to compromise our obedience to God?

SCRIPTURE AND STUDY MANUAL

(45 minutes adults)   (30 minutes youth)
Form three groups to look for the big picture in Revelation. Group 1—Days 1 and 3; Group 2—Day 2; Group 3—Days 4 and 5. Work through each day's Scripture and notes to identify and list—without interpreting or explaining—images, pictures, and symbolic language. Consider the list and discuss these questions: What big picture emerges from these details? What is the overarching message?

In the total group recall the difference between *prophetic* and *apocalyptic* from study manual page 212. Then study Old Testament examples of apocalyptic writing with themes similar to those in Revelation. Work in three groups: Group 1—Isaiah 24–27; Group 2—Ezekiel 38–39; Group 3—Daniel 7–12. Scan the passages looking for such themes as heavenly signs, judgment, signs pointing to end time, the final victory of God's people. Discuss this question: How do these themes and images convey the message that God is in control of history?

Revelation repeatedly pictures the struggle of the church and its eventual victory over the world. Form pairs or threes and assign one passage to each: Revelation 1:9–5:14; 6–11; 12–16; 17:1–22:5. Scan assigned passages with these questions in mind: Where and how is the church's struggle pictured? What is John saying to the church? What promises of victory over the world does John give the church? Hear from each group.

Hear any "If You Want to Know More" reports.

BREAK

(10 minutes)

ENCOUNTER THE WORD

(35 minutes adults)   (15 minutes youth)
Scripture selection: Revelation 4
Hear Revelation 4 read aloud with eyes closed. Then read the passage silently, listing sounds, smells, sights, touches, tastes. Talk through the passage and lists with a partner and then with another pair. Discuss this question: What insights did you get from reading Scripture this way? Sing "Holy, Holy, Holy." (See using all the senses in Bible study, pages 57–61 of *Teaching the Bible to Adults and Youth*.)

MARKS OF FAITHFUL COMMUNITY

(20 minutes)
Being faithful community, we live and work in the present, expecting God's victory in the future, secure in knowing the end—whenever it comes—is in God's hands.

Read "Our Human Condition." In fours compare the views of life expressed there and in written responses to the first question in this section. Read the mark of faithful community. In discussing the last two questions, consider "The Radical Disciple" statement.

CLOSING AND PRAYER

(5 minutes adults)   (10 minutes youth)
Turn to Lesson 28 and check assignments. Write down prayer concerns. Close by praying Psalm 2.

28 Letters to the Churches

In case you've delayed, order the *DISCIPLE: UNDER THE TREE OF LIFE Revelation Video Letter* for Session 31 immediately. See teacher helps page 12 for description of the letter and ordering procedure.

GATHERING AND PRAYER

(5 minutes)

VIDEO SEGMENT 28

(20 minutes)
Presenter: Catherine Gunsalus González
Scripture: Marquis Laughlin

Prepare to View Video

Listen for the setting of the churches, the temptations to compromise Christian identity and loyalty.

View Video

Summary of video content:

The cities are in the province of Asia, the heart of wealth and population of the Roman Empire.

Faithful Jews and Christians suffer sporadic persecutions for their loyalty to God.

The issue is how these Christian communities can maintain their identity and not give the empire their highest loyalty.

Discuss After Viewing Video

What forms did the temptation to compromise Christian identity and loyalty take? What compromises of faith do we make to live in society?

SCRIPTURE AND STUDY MANUAL

(50 minutes adults)   (35 minutes youth)

The vision of the letters to the seven churches establishes a context in which to understand the visions that come later in Revelation. Form four groups to study the vision of the seven churches. Each group will study Scripture for Day 1 plus Scripture for one other day: Group 1—Days 1 and 2; Group 2—Days 1 and 3; Group 3—Days 1 and 4; Group 4—Days 1 and 5. All groups will follow the same steps in working with their assigned Scriptures: (1) Refer to Scripture for Day 1 to establish the situation in which John received the vision and the Christ of his vision. (2) Answer these questions: What light do the passages from other parts of the Bible throw on the assigned Revelation passage? What is the message in the letter to this church?

(3) Draw on information in the study manual about the church and about the city to answer this question: What cultural influences did the church have to contend with? (4) What message to this church is applicable to the church in every age and location?

Now in the total group hear responses to the question at the top of study manual page 221.

To get a glimpse of the Christ of John's vision, in groups of three or four read the italicized verse that introduces each church beginning on study manual page 216 and talk about what each verse tells us about Christ.

BREAK

(10 minutes)

ENCOUNTER THE WORD

(40 minutes adults)   (20 minutes youth)
Scripture selection: Colossians 1:9-23

Hear Colossians 1:9-23 read aloud. In groups of three or four study the passage using these questions: What does the passage say? What does it intend to communicate? As twenty-first century people, what do we say to this passage? What does God say to me through this passage? (See dialogue and encounter, pages 51–56 of *Teaching the Bible to Adults and Youth.*)

MARKS OF FAITHFUL COMMUNITY

(20 minutes)

Being faithful community, we listen to what the Spirit of God is saying to our congregation and strive to be faithful.

Read "Our Human Condition" aloud without comment. Then in two groups, hear responses to the three questions in this section. Read the mark of faithful community. What do you hear the Spirit of God saying to your congregation? Look now at "The Radical Disciple." What pull toward accommodation and compromise is being experienced in your congregation? How would radical disciples call the congregation to accountability and faithfulness?

CLOSING AND PRAYER

(5 minutes adults)   (10 minutes youth)

Turn to Lesson 29 and check assignments. Note the "Psalm of the Week." Write down prayer concerns. Close by praying Psalm 86:1-11 aloud.

29 What Must Take Place

GATHERING AND PRAYER

(5 minutes)

VIDEO SEGMENT 29

(20 minutes)
Presenter: Leonard Thompson
Scripture: Marquis Laughlin

Prepare to View Video

Listen for recurring images, conflict between church and society, divine deliverance and renewal.

View Video

Summary of video content:
John writes in the concrete images of poetry.
John weaves images together to create a surplus of meaning.
John warns Christians not to be deceived; a benign empire masks satanic, beastly powers.
John's visions present church and society in an irreconcilable conflict—Christ against culture.
John never loses faith in the power of divine deliverance and cosmic renewal.

Discuss After Viewing Video

How does John weave images together to create a surplus of meaning? What forms does the conflict between church and society take in the visions? What images of divine deliverance and renewal does John provide?

SCRIPTURE AND STUDY MANUAL

(50 minutes adults)   (35 minutes youth)

Try to approach the vision of God and the Lamb in Revelation 4–5 with the awe John must have felt. In groups of three or four reflect on your experience of these chapters using these questions: What sense did you get of John's reaction to what he saw and heard? What were your feelings as you read the chapters? When did you find yourself thinking, I know about that? I know what that term or image means? I recognize that scriptural language? When did you experience worship as you read?

Explore the message in the scenes presented in Scriptures for Days 2–5. Remind the group that much of the mystery of Revelation remains hidden in images, language, and symbols beyond ordinary thought and experience. Form two groups and make these assignments: Group 1—Days 2 and 3; Group 2—Days 4 and 5. Instruct the groups to study the Scriptures not so much to explain symbolic language or images but to ask what function or purpose the symbols, images, and language serve in the overall message of Revelation. To assist their discussion, groups may refer to daily notes and related sections in the study manual and consult annotations and footnotes in their study Bibles.

The "Psalm of the Week" offers another picture of the exalted Lord. Read Psalm 97 in unison. Invite persons who wrote a litany as suggested in the "Psalm of the Week" to read their litanies and if possible to involve the group in the litanies.

BREAK

(10 minutes)

ENCOUNTER THE WORD

(40 minutes adults)   (20 minutes youth)
Scripture selection: Revelation 7

Ask one person to read the narrative sections of Revelation 7 aloud and the group to join on the poetry sections. In groups of three or four study the chapter with these questions in mind: What does this passage tell us about God? about men and women? about the relationship between God and human beings? (See theological Bible study, pages 40–41 of *Teaching the Bible to Adults and Youth*.)

MARKS OF FAITHFUL COMMUNITY

(20 minutes)

Being faithful community, we refuse to be defined and confined by the routine; we take our place in the universal struggle, knowing that victory is assured.

Read "Our Human Condition." According to this statement, what determines life's priorities? Read the mark of faithful community. What determines the priorities of faithful community?

In groups of three or four hear responses to the questions in this section of the study manual.

Finally, in pairs read "The Radical Disciple" and say what makes perseverance in praying radical. Say how you might become a powerful person of prayer.

CLOSING AND PRAYER

(5 minutes adults)   (10 minutes youth)

Turn to Lesson 30 and check assignments. Write down prayer concerns. Close with prayer.

30 The Power of Evil

GATHERING AND PRAYER

(5 minutes)

VIDEO SEGMENT 30

(25 minutes)
Presenter: Justo L. González
Scripture: Marquis Laughlin

Prepare to View Video

Listen for what is said about what the book of Revelation is and what it is not, for what is said about the fulfillment of God's purposes.

View Video

Summary of video content:

God's revelation is telling us something clearly enough so that we are called to obedience.

The book of Revelation was the Word of God when it was written; it is still the Word of God.

If we read Revelation as it is intended, as poetry, as imagery that refers to the deepest truths of human life, it not only makes sense; it moves us.

The message of Revelation is that God's purposes in history will be fulfilled.

Discuss After Viewing Video

How are we to read the book of Revelation? In reading Revelation, what has assured you God's purposes will be fulfilled?

SCRIPTURE AND STUDY MANUAL

(50 minutes adults)   (35 minutes youth)

Several themes weave their way in recurring fashion through Revelation 13–18. Crucial to hearing this Scripture is the recognition that Christians cannot think of themselves as neutral onlookers but must see themselves in the midst of the conflict being called to repent, resist, endure. Representative of the recurring themes are these: *the combination of warning and promise; the urgency of endurance; the call to faithfulness; divine wrath as warning; hints of the outcome of the conflict; God's grace in already having claimed us; the great city "Babylon" is not confined to one time or place; the way ahead is through the persecution, not around it.* In two groups talk through Revelation 13–18 a chapter at a time looking for recurring themes and how they are expressed. Provide or display the list of themes to guide review and to prompt discussion.

Then respond to the questions on study manual pages 235 and 237.

BREAK

(10 minutes)

ENCOUNTER THE WORD

(35 minutes adults)   (15 minutes youth)
Scripture selection: Revelation 13; 4–5

Last week's reading assignments included Revelation 4–5. Revelation 13, in this week's reading assignments, is a counterpoint or contrast to Revelation 4–5. Form two groups to contrast the temporal power represented by the Roman Empire in Revelation 13 with divine power represented by God and the Lamb in Chapters 4–5. In the groups begin by reading Chapter 13, followed by reading Chapters 4–5. Look for contrasts in power. What differences do you see in tone and feeling, in the way the two kinds of power are expressed?

MARKS OF FAITHFUL COMMUNITY

(20 minutes)

Being faithful community, we choose to be faithful rather than fearful, bold in our witness whatever the cost.

Consider "Our Human Condition," Revelation 18:4-5, and the mark of faithful community together. Follow the pattern of read, reflect, talk. Read "Our Human Condition." What do you think? Read Revelation 18:4-5. What do you think? Read the mark of faithful community. What do you think? What message do you hear when you consider these three statements together? Now discuss the two questions in this section of the study manual.

Call attention to "The Radical Disciple." Knowing who is suffering for their faith is not always easy. Talk in the total group about who might need your support and how to offer it.

CLOSING AND PRAYER

(5 minutes adults)   (10 minutes youth)

Turn to Lesson 31 and check assignments. Remind the group of the longer length of Sessions 31 and 32. Begin making the necessary arrangements for those sessions. Write down prayer concerns. Close by praying the daily prayer on study manual page 230.

31 A New Heaven and a New Earth

Note to the teacher: Because this session ends in silence, make necessary arrangements and give instructions about the love feast in Session 32 before you begin this session. Notice the difference in content, sequence, and time of this session. Plan for at least three and one-half hours.

GATHERING AND PRAYER

(5 minutes)

SCRIPTURE AND STUDY MANUAL

(50 minutes adults)   (35 minutes youth)

To get an overall sense of the teachings in this week's Scripture—*martyrs, Satan, Christ, thrones of judgment, first resurrection, books and final judgment, lake of fire, second death, marriage supper, new Jerusalem, the water of life and the tree of life, God and the Lamb*—in threes or fours work through Scripture and daily notes for Days 1–4 one day at a time. Use these questions to guide discussion: What images did you see? What words did you hear? What mystery do you experience? What vocabulary in words and images has the Scripture given you that equips you for the experiences of life and death?

John includes seven beatitudes (blesseds) in Revelation—1:3; 14:13; 16:15; 19:9; 20:6; 22:7, 14. In pairs read the beatitudes and talk about how these beatitudes carry the story line or message in Revelation.

Twice John is reproved for attempting to worship an angel. Why? Read Revelation 19:10; 22:8-9 in the total group and discuss these questions: How do these reproofs fit into the overall message of Revelation? What is the temptation here for us?

Listen to the guidance from Jesus and John. Individually scan "Presumption," study manual pages 245–246, to identify guidance from Jesus and John important to you. Then talk with a partner. Now join another pair and respond to the question on study manual page 246.

Psalm of the week. Divide Psalm 148 among group members and read it aloud with joy.

ENCOUNTER THE WORD

(40 minutes adults)   (20 minutes youth)

Scripture selection: Matthew 25:31-46

Invite someone to read Matthew 25:31-46 aloud while others follow along in their Bibles. In groups of three or four discuss these questions: What event is described in the passage? How is it to take place? What does the passage intend to communicate? What does it say? Allow ten minutes for discussion. Now read the passage again silently and in the same groups discuss these questions one at a time: What do I say? As twenty-first century people, what do we say to this text? Allow ten minutes for discussion. Again, hear the passage read aloud and discuss these questions one at a time: What does God say to me? How am I involved in the event described? What claim does this passage place on me? (See dialogue and encounter, pages 51–56 of *Teaching the Bible to Adults and Youth*.)

MARKS OF FAITHFUL COMMUNITY

(20 minutes)

Being faithful community, we live fully in the present, confronting the evil that surrounds us, and fully in the promise of God's new heaven and new earth.

Read the first paragraph in the study manual under "Marks of Faithful Community" silently and respond in the total group to the first question in this section. Now read aloud "Our Human Condition," the mark of faithful community, and "The Radical Disciple." In groups of three or four pick one evidence of evil mentioned in "Our Human Condition" and consider the "small" related day-to-day evils we know but have come to tolerate. What do you see and participate in daily that you recognize as evil—evil you have power to stand against? evil you can act on without waiting for anyone else to act? responsibilities against evil you can't place on someone else? End the discussion by speaking individual laments. Begin with the words *Lord, I lament . . . .*

BREAK

(10 minutes)

THE REVELATION: A WORSHIP EXPERIENCE

(90 minutes)

Introduce the video experience after the break and before moving to the video room. Briefly make these points:

1. The Revelation video's challenge to DISCIPLE participants: Refer to the five points identified by dots on teacher helps page 11.

2. The video experience of worship is not a formally structured worship service. Refer to the information in the second paragraph on teacher helps page 11.
3. Drama, art, spoken words, music, metaphor, and symbol characterize this video. Mention that the group's familiarity with the language and images of Revelation prepares them to make connections in what they see and hear. And like the book of Revelation, the video will evoke a variety of emotions.
4. During this video-led worship experience, group members will sing, speak, listen, pray, offer laments and pleas for mercy. The video worship leader will guide their participation. You will take the lead in group response and they are to follow your lead.
5. The video stays on the entire time.
6. The video concludes with the instruction "Go in silence." Encourage everyone to honor the silence.
7. Mention the names of three persons directly related to *The Revelation: A Worship Experience:*
   Dennis Parlato—experienced in film, television, and theater, video worship leader in *The Revelation: A Worship Experience.*
   Mac Pirkle—President of Southern Stage Productions, a theatrical production company, Nashville, Tennessee, writer and creative director, and the second speaker in the video.
   Don Saliers—Parker Professor of Theology and Worship, Candler School of Theology, Emory University, consultant and co-writer on the liturgical moments.
8. Invite the group to move now to the room where the video will be shown.

ADVANCE PREPARATION FOR THE VIDEO

1. Read the total plan for Session 31, teacher helps pages 60–61 to see how *The Revelation: A Worship Experience* fits into the whole session.

2. Plan for the session to take three and one-half hours because the video takes ninety minutes.

3. Read teacher helps pages 11–13, *The Revelation: A Worship Experience.*

4. Preview the video. You will need at least one and a half hours to preview it and make notes. Use the guide for viewing on teacher helps pages 11–13 for making notes about your responsibilities and the pace of the video.

5. Make arrangements for the room for showing the video. If at all possible, it should be a room different from where the study and discussion part of the session takes place.

6. Locate the Revelation video letter (which you should have ordered and received by now) to be used during the video. Do not break the seal.

7. Gather seven candles plus a taper and matches to light the candles, a table for the candles, and a cloth to drape the table.

8. Decide the room arrangement—placement of the television monitor, the table with the candles, and a semicircle of chairs in front of the television.

9. Check the television monitor and videocassette recorder to be sure they are working properly.

10. Cue the videotape.

32 Under the Tree of Life

Note to the teacher: In addition to study and discussion of Scripture and video, this session includes a love feast with footwashing, fellowship meal, and Holy Communion. Plan for a session of approximately three and one-half to four hours.

GATHERING AND PRAYER

(5 minutes)

SCRIPTURE AND STUDY MANUAL

(50 minutes adults)   (35 minutes youth)

Review Scripture and discuss the related questions in the study manual. Follow the same pattern for each day: Review Scripture and daily notes in fours and discuss related questions in pairs. Each group will work with Scripture and questions for all five days. Allow about seven minutes per day.

Day 1—Review Scripture and notes to remind one another what the different passages are about and how caring was expressed or taught in the various passages. Respond to the questions on "Caring," study manual page 250.

Day 2—Review Scripture and notes to identify examples of guidance and summarize specific guidance. Respond to the questions on "Guidance," study manual pages 250–251.

Day 3—Review Scripture and notes to clarify what sort of building is spoken about in the passages. Respond to the questions on "Building," study manual pages 251–252.

Day 4—Review Scripture and notes and discuss this question: What new perspectives on yourself and on life do these passages provide you? Form new pairs to discuss the questions on "Humility," study manual pages 252–253.

Day 5—Review Scripture and notes and discuss this question: What for you is the basis for hope according to each of these passages? Respond to the questions on "Hope," study manual page 253.

Read aloud "Our Human Condition" and the mark of faithful community. Respond to these questions: What connection do you see between vulnerability and obedience? What contrast between control and the yielded life? What solution to the human condition do you hear in the image of a God who stooped to wash feet?

Invite persons to reflect on the radical disciple described throughout this study and to suggest one word that sums up the radical disciple.

Stand and read Psalm 96 aloud together. Pause at various points for two or three brief voluntary responses: After verse 3 tell of God's day-to-day salvation; after verse 6 name idols powerless before this God; after verse 9 give glory and praise to God.

ENCOUNTER THE WORD

(40 minutes adults)   (20 minutes youth)
Scripture selection: John 15:1-8

Hear John 15:1-8 read aloud. Study the passage individually for about five minutes with these questions in mind: What does the passage say? What do you think Jesus intended his disciples to hear? What do Jesus' words say to the church today? Then in groups of three or four discuss the questions one at a time. Read the passage silently and reflect on this question: If I take this passage seriously, what changes will I have to make in my life? Talk in pairs. (See depth Bible study, pages 35–39 of *Teaching the Bible to Adults and Youth*.)

BREAK

(10 minutes)

VIDEO SEGMENT 32

(20 minutes)
Presenters: Richard B. Wilke, Julia K. Wilke

Prepare to View Video

This video segment prepares the group for the love feast. No discussion follows the video.

View Video
Summary of video content:

Wisdom is a way of thinking consequentially.
The Scriptures are wisdom, a tree of life.
The tree of life stands for God's original plan—a world before greed and selfishness set in.
The cross of Jesus symbolizes the tree of life that held the sacrifice that will save us and lead us to eternal life.
We wash other people's feet because Jesus did.

THE LOVE FEAST

(90–120 minutes)

Give necessary instructions and move into the love feast. The "Sending Forth" at the end of the love feast will bring to a close your study of DISCIPLE.

ADVANCE PREPARATION FOR LOVE FEAST

1. Read the explanation and order of the love feast, study manual pages 254–256.

2. Read "The Love Feast," teacher helps page 14.

3. Decide who will read Scripture and take other leadership roles during the love feast. Contact them prior to the session.

4. Gather hymnals for use during the service.

5. Decide if the footwashing will be done in silence or while the group sings quietly. Choose songs and invite someone in the group to start the songs.

6. Know the procedure for footwashing. At the designated time in the service, the leader takes the towel, basin, and pitcher of water, kneels before the person to his or her left, places the basin on the floor, pours water over the person's feet, one foot at a time, and dries one foot at a time. Appropriate signs of peace—the words *God bless you,* an embrace, or handclasp—follow the washing and drying of a person's feet. The one whose feet have been washed repeats the process for the person to the left. Continue around the circle until the leader who began the footwashing has her or his feet washed.

Instruct persons ahead of time to wear sandals or shoes and socks, no hose. Some persons may be uncomfortable participating in the footwashing. Offer the washing of hands as an alternative. The process would be similar: Wash and dry the hands one at a time and give expressions of peace and love. Indicate early that any person is welcome simply to observe rather than to participate in the footwashing.

7. With your group members in mind, make any necessary adjustments in the footwashing procedure that might prove awkward or embarrassing, or affect a person's ability to participate fully. Plan furniture arrangement to accommodate persons who may not be able to stoop or kneel.

8. Gather items for the footwashing: a basin, pitchers of warm water, towels (if you prefer, towels large enough to tie around the waist and use for drying the feet, as in Jesus' example, John 13:4). Provide another basin, pitchers of warm water, hand soap, and towels for washing hands afterward.

9. Decide space and equipment needs. So that participants may experience the sense of community, unity, and wholeness that mark the love feast, arrange for the footwashing, fellowship meal, and Holy Communion to take place in the same room. Moving from one room to another tends to break both the flow of the service and the sense of worship.

Keep in mind also that the first two hours of the session follow the weekly pattern of study, discussion, and viewing the video. Arrange for space and equipment for these activities.

10. Agree on menu and responsibility for food.

11. Make the necessary arrangements for Holy Communion.

DISCIPLE Group Members

Name _____   Address _____

            Phone _____

Name _____   Address _____

            Phone _____

Name _____   Address _____

            Phone _____

Name _____   Address _____

            Phone _____

Name _____   Address _____

            Phone _____

Name _____   Address _____

            Phone _____

Name _____   Address _____

            Phone _____

Name _____   Address _____

            Phone _____

Name _____   Address _____

            Phone _____

Name _____   Address _____

            Phone _____

Name _____   Address _____

            Phone _____

Name _____   Address _____

            Phone _____

Name _____   Address _____

            Phone _____